CONTENTS

➤ STUDENT JOURNAL

Paths to College and Career
English Language Arts

Working with Evidence

Published by Jossey-Bass
A Wiley Brand
One Montgomery Street, Suite 1000, San Francisco, CA 94104-4594—www.josseybass.com

Jossey-Bass books and products are available through most bookstores. To contact Jossey-Bass directly call our Customer Care Department within the U.S. at 800-956-7739, outside the U.S. at 317-572-3986, or fax 317-572-4002.

Wiley publishes in a variety of print and electronic formats and by print-on-demand. Some material included with standard print versions of this book may not be included in e-books or in print-on-demand. If this book refers to media such as a CD or DVD that is not included in the version you purchased, you may download this material at http://booksupport.wiley.com. For more information about Wiley products, visit www.wiley.com.

ISBN: 978-1-119-10567-1

Printed in the United States of America

FIRST EDITION
PB Printing   B10002978_080718

Unit 2   109

Unit 3   188

Taking a Stand

Gallery Walk

women war protestors

http://www.loc.gov/pictures/resource/hec.28132/

protestors in hall

http://www.loc.gov/pictures/resource/npcc.18539/

suffragists

http://www.loc.gov/item/mnwp000288

jewish demonstrators

http://lcweb2.loc.gov/service/pnp/ppmsca/06500/06591v.jpg

civil rights march

http://www.loc.gov/pictures/item/2003654393/

Notice/Wonder Note-Catcher

Notice	Wonder

Taking a Stand: Frayer Model

Name: _____

Date: _____

Definition	Characteristics/Explanation
Examples	**Nonexamples**

EXPEDITIONARY
LEARNING

T-chart: Advantages/Disadvantages

Name: _____

Date: _____

Taking a Stand Photographs	
What are the advantages of using a photograph to learn about taking a stand? How is it positive or helpful?	What are the disadvantages of using a photograph to learn about taking a stand? How is it negative or unhelpful?

"Equal Rights for Women"

Shirley Chisholm. "Equal Rights for Women." Address to the United States House of Representatives, Washington, DC, May 21, 1969. Public domain.

Hon. Shirley Chisholm of New York

In the House of Representatives, May 21, 1969

Mr. Speaker,

When a young woman graduates from college and starts looking for a job, she is likely to have a frustrating and even demeaning* experience ahead of her. If she walks into an office for an interview, the first question she will be asked is, "Do you type?"

There is a calculated system of prejudice that lies unspoken behind that question. Why is it acceptable for women to be secretaries, librarians, and teachers, but totally unacceptable for them to be managers, administrators, doctors, lawyers, and Members of Congress?

The unspoken assumption is that women are different. They do not have executive ability, orderly minds, stability, leadership skills, and they are too emotional.

It has been observed before that society for a long time discriminated against another minority, the blacks, on the same basis—that they were different and inferior. The happy little homemaker and the contented "old darkey"* on the plantation were both produced by prejudice.

As a black person, I am no stranger to race prejudice. But the truth is that in the political world I have been far oftener discriminated against because I am a woman than because I am black.

Prejudice against blacks is becoming unacceptable although it will take years to eliminate it. But it is doomed because, slowly, white America is beginning to admit that it exists. Prejudice against women is still acceptable. There is very little understanding yet of the immorality* involved in double pay scales and the classification of most of the better jobs as "for men only."

More than half of the population of the United States is female. But women occupy only 2 percent of the managerial positions. They have not even reached the level of tokenism* yet. No women sit on the AFL-CIO council or Supreme Court. There have been only two women who have held Cabinet rank, and at present there are none. Only two women now hold ambassadorial rank in the diplomatic corps. In Congress, we are down to one Senator and 10 Representatives.

Considering that there are about 3 1/2 million more women in the United States than men, this situation is outrageous.

It is true that part of the problem has been that women have not been aggressive in demanding their rights. This was also true of the black population for many years. They submitted to oppression* and even cooperated with it. Women have done the same thing. But now there is an awareness of this situation particularly among the younger segment of the population.

As in the field of equal rights for blacks, Spanish-Americans, the Indians, and other groups, laws will not change such deep-seated problems overnight. But they can be used to provide protection for those who are most abused, and to begin the process of evolutionary* change by compelling the insensitive majority to reexamine its unconscious* attitudes.

It is for this reason that I wish to introduce today a proposal that has been before every Congress for the last 40 years and that sooner or later must become part of the basic law of the land—the equal rights amendment.

Let me note and try to refute two of the commonest arguments that are offered against this amendment. One is that women are already protected under the law and do not need legislation. Existing laws are not adequate to secure equal rights for women. Sufficient proof of this is the concentration of women in lower-paying, menial,* unrewarding jobs and their incredible scarcity in the upper-level jobs. If women are already equal, why is it such an event whenever one happens to be elected to Congress?

It is obvious that discrimination exists. Women do not have the opportunities that men do. And women that do not conform to the system, who try to break with the accepted patterns, are stigmatized as "odd" and "unfeminine." The fact is that a woman who aspires to be chairman of the board, or a Member of the House, does so for exactly the same reasons as any man. Basically, these are that she thinks she can do the job and she wants to try.

A second argument often heard against the equal rights amendment is that it would eliminate legislation that many States and the Federal Government have enacted giving special protection to women and that it would throw the marriage and divorce laws into chaos.

As for the marriage laws, they are due for a sweeping* reform, and an excellent beginning would be to wipe the existing ones off the books. Regarding special protection for working women, I cannot understand why it should be needed. Women need no protection that men do not need. What we need are laws to protect working people, to guarantee them fair pay, safe working conditions, protection against sickness and layoffs, and provision for dignified, comfortable retirement.

Men and women need these things equally. That one sex needs protection more than the other is a male supremacist* myth as ridiculous and unworthy of respect as the white supremacist myths that society is trying to cure itself of at this time.

*demeaning: humiliating

"old darkey": a derogatory and racist name for African Americans used in the early 1900s

immorality: without moral principles

tokenism: a policy of making only a symbolic effort, but not really meaning it

oppression: unjust or cruel power

evolutionary: gradual

unconscious: unaware

menial: lowly, unskilled

Reading Closely: Guiding Questions

APPROACHING TEXTS

Reading closely begins by considering my specific purposes for reading and important information about a text.

I am aware of my purposes for reading:

- Why am I reading this text?
- In my reading, should I focus on:
  ⇨ The content and information about the topic?
  ⇨ The structure and language of the text?
  ⇨ The author's view?

I take note of information about the text:

- What is the title?
- Who is the author?
- What type of text is it?
- Who published the text?
- When was the text published?

QUESTIONING TEXTS

Reading closely involves:

1. Initially questioning a text to focus my attention on its structure, ideas, language, and perspective

THEN

2. Questioning further as I read to sharpen my focus on the specific details in the text

I begin my reading with questions to help me understand the text, and I pose new questions while reading that help me deepen my understanding:

Structure:

- How is the text organized?
- How has the author structured the sentences, lines, paragraphs, scenes, or stanzas?

Topic, Information, and Ideas:

- What information/ideas are presented at the beginning of the text?
- What stands out to me as I first examine this text?
- What information/ideas are described in detail?
- What do I learn about the topic as I read?
- How do the ideas relate to what I already know?
- What do I think this text is mainly about?

Language:

- What words or phrases stand out to me as I read?
- What words and phrases are powerful or unique?
- What do the author's words cause me to see or feel?
- What words do I need to define to better understand the text?
- What words and phrases are repeated?

Perspective:

- Who is the intended audience of the text?
- What is the author's/narrator's stance or attitude about the topic or theme?
- How does the author's language show his or her perspective?
- What is the author's personal relationship to the topic or themes?

ANALYZING DETAILS

Reading closely involves analyzing and connecting the details I have found through my questioning to determine their meaning and importance, and the ways they help develop ideas across a text.

I analyze the details I find through my questioning:

Patterns across the text:

- What does the repetition of words or phrases in the text suggest?
- How do details, information, characters, or ideas change across the text?
- How do the text's structure and features influence my reading?

Meaning of language:

- How do specific words or phrases affect the meaning of the text?
- What words or phrases are critical for my understanding of the text?

Importance:

- Which details are most important to the overall meaning of the text?
- Which sections are most challenging and require closer reading?

Relationships among details:

- How are details in the text related in a way that develops themes or ideas?
- What does the text leave uncertain or unstated? Why?

"Reading Closely for Details: Guiding Questions," by Odell Education – www.odelleducation.com – Copyright (2014) by Odell Education. Used with permission from Odell Education.

EXPEDITIONARY
LEARNING

"Equal Rights for Women"

Lesson 2 Text-Dependent Questions

Name: _____

Date: _____

Approaching the Text	Notes
Who is the author?	
What is the title?	
What type of text is it?	
Who is the audience?	

Read the text silently in your head as you hear it read aloud.

Text-Dependent Questions	Notes
1. What is prejudice?	
2. According to Shirley Chisholm, what are the assumptions of the "calculated system of prejudice" that lies behind the question, "Do you type?"	

3. Look at paragraph 4. What does Chisholm mean by the "happy little homemaker"? What does Chisholm mean by the "contented 'old darkey'"?	
4. Look at paragraphs 5–6. What similarities and differences does Chisholm see between the experience of women and that of blacks?	
5. Look at paragraphs 7 and 8. What are the various statistics Chisholm uses to support her argument?	
6. Choose one statistic and use your own words to explain what it means.	

Instructions for Discussion Appointments

Make one appointment at each location.

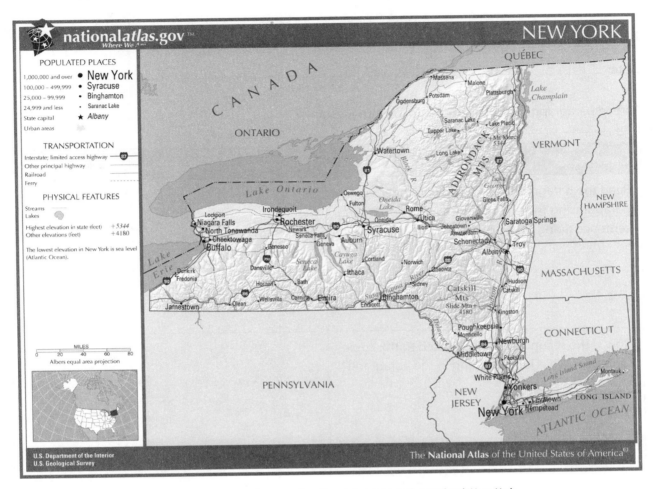

Source: United States Geological Survey, http://nationalmap.gov/small_scale/printable/reference.html#New_York

In Albany:	
In Buffalo:	
In New York City:	
In Rochester:	

"Equal Rights for Women"

Analyzing Text Structure Note-Catcher

Name: Michael J Polsett

Date: 11/22/19

Reread paragraph 9 and answer the following questions:

Questions	Notes
Read the paragraph aloud with your peer. Try paraphrasing the first sentence. What job is this sentence doing in the paragraph?	Woman havent been very assresive.
How is the second sentence related to this topic sentence? What job is it doing in the paragraph?	fight for woman rights
Now look at the third sentence, beginning with "They submitted . . ." Who are "they"? What do you think *submitted* means? Now that you know this, see if you can figure out what job this sentence is doing in the paragraph.	I think "they" are Men I Think Submitted Means to accect

M

| In the next sentence, what does the "same thing" refer to? What job is this sentence doing in the paragraph? | Woman have bobo what mea do |
| With your peer, paraphrase the last sentence. How does this sentence relate to the first sentence of the paragraph? Why do you think the author ends the paragraph this way? | to end the Parbagrah strongly |

Evaluating Evidence Note-Catcher

Name: _____

Date: _____

Claim	What piece of evidence does Chisholm use to best support that argument?	Why is that the best piece of evidence?

Summary Writing Graphic Organizer

Name: _____

Date: _____

- When you are reading actively, one of the most important things you do is figure out what the point of it is. This means you recognize the controlling idea of the text.

- Once you have done that, you have really done the hardest part of the work.

- Still, there is more! You need to figure out what the key details in the text are and write a great closing sentence, a clincher.

- Once that is done, you are ready to write up the notes into a summary paragraph. At that point, you will have gotten a good, basic understanding of the text you are reading.

Controlling Idea

Key detail	Key detail	Key detail

Key detail	Key detail	Key detail

Clincher

"Equal Rights for Women"

Close Reading Note-Catcher

Name: _Michael J Polnett_

Date: _11/25/19_

Chalk Talk Questions	Notes
1. What is Shirley Chisholm thinking and saying about discrimination against women?	They are experiencing discrimination in the force
2. Who is the intended audience for this speech?	The house of representatives
3. What is Shirley Chisholm's personal role in discrimination against women?	She advocates For Womens rights.
4. Reread the speech. Where does Chisholm acknowledge other viewpoints?	Part 5 - Paragraph one
5. How does Chisholm respond to these other viewpoints?	refute - Prove them wrong
6. Why does Chisholm identify other viewpoints?	to make an arguement stonger

"Equal Rights for Women"

Vocabulary

Name: _____

Date: _____

Directions: In the following chart, write the words you circled in "Equal Rights for Women." Do your best to infer the meaning of the word from the context and write it in the second column. Then, using a dictionary, check your inferred meaning and write the dictionary definition in the third column.

Word	Paragraph Number	Inferred Meaning	Dictionary Definition

"Ain't I a Woman?"

Sojourner Truth

Source: Sojourner Truth. "Ain't I a Woman?" Speech delivered at the Women's Rights Convention, Akron, Ohio, 1851. This version was recounted by Frances Gage in 1863. Public domain.

Well, children, where there is so much racket* there must be something out of kilter.* I think that 'twixt the negroes of the South and the women at the North, all talking about rights, the white men will be in a fix pretty soon. But what's all this here talking about?

That man over there says that women need to be helped into carriages, and lifted over ditches, and to have the best place everywhere. Nobody ever helps me into carriages, or over mud puddles, or gives me any best place! And ain't I a woman? Look at me! Look at my arm! I have ploughed and planted, and gathered into barns, and no man could head me! And ain't I a woman? I could work as much and eat as much as a man—when I could get it—and bear the lash* as well! And ain't I a woman? I have borne thirteen children, and seen most all sold off to slavery, and when I cried out with my mother's grief, none but Jesus heard me! And ain't I a woman?

Then they talk about this thing in the head; what's this they call it? [member of audience whispers, "intellect"] That's it, honey. What's that got to do with women's rights or negroes' rights? If my cup won't hold but a pint, and yours holds a quart, wouldn't you be mean not to let me have my little half measure full?

Then that little man in black there, he says women can't have as much rights as men, 'cause Christ wasn't a woman! Where did your Christ come from? Where did your Christ come from? From God and a woman! Man had nothing to do with Him.

If the first woman God ever made was strong enough to turn the world upside down all alone, these women together ought to be able to turn it back, and get it right side up again! And now they is asking to do it, the men better let them.

Obliged* to you for hearing me, and now old Sojourner ain't got nothing more to say.

racket: noise

out of kilter: unbalanced

bear the lash: handle pain; but literally, in the context of slavery, survive a whipping

obliged: I appreciate and owe you

"Ain't I a Woman?" Note-Catcher

Name: _____

Date: _____

Round 1: Finding the central idea and supporting details	Round 2: Analyzing text structure
According to Truth, what is the "fix" that white men are in? What details does Truth use to support that idea?	What objection to women having rights is Truth addressing here? How does each sentence in the paragraph contribute to Truth's response to that?

Round 3: Analyzing perspective and opposing claim	Summary Preparation
What stand is Sojourner Truth taking in this speech?	What is the controlling idea?
What opposing claim does Truth address in this speech? How does she respond?	What are the key details?
	What is your clincher?

Homework: Write an objective summary of "Ain't I a Woman?"

EXPEDITIONARY
LEARNING

Mid-Unit Assessment

Analyzing Excerpts from Lyndon Johnson's Speech "The Great Society"

Name: _____

Date: _____

Directions: Read the excerpts from President Johnson's speech, then reread the speech and write the gist of each part of the speech in the column to the right.

President Lyndon B. Johnson gave this speech at the University of Michigan's graduation ceremony on May 22, 1964. He directed his speech primarily to the students who were graduating that day.

Excerpts from Speech	Gist
Part 1 *self motivated* Your imagination and your initiative and your indignation[1] will determine whether we build a society where progress is the servant of our needs, or a society where old values and new visions are buried under unbridled[2] growth. For in your time we have the opportunity to move not only toward the rich society and the powerful society, but upward to the Great Society. The Great Society rests on abundance and liberty for all. It demands an end to poverty and racial injustice, to which we are totally committed in our time. But that is just the beginning. So I want to talk to you today about three places where we begin to build the Great Society— in our cities, in our countryside, and in our classrooms.	it's trying to telling about how we are the inscredent to are society we get to choose eather we want to build & Progress or have old values & new visions are buried under unbridled W
Part 2 Aristotle[3] said: "Men come together in cities in order to live, but they remain together in order to live the good life." It is harder and harder to	

live the good life in American cities today. The catalog of ills[4] is long: There is the decay of the centers and the despoiling[5] of the suburbs. There is not enough housing for our people or transportation for our traffic. Open land is vanishing and old landmarks are violated. Worst of all, expansion is eroding these precious and time-honored values of community with neighbors and communion[6] with nature. The loss of these values breeds loneliness and boredom and indifference.

And our society will never be great until our cities are great. Today the frontier of imagination and innovation is inside those cities. . . . New experiments are already going on. It will be the task of your generation to make the American city a place where future generations will come, not only to live, but to live the good life.

Part 3

A second place where we begin to build the Great Society is in our countryside. We have always prided ourselves on being not only America the strong and America the free, but America the beautiful. Today that beauty is in danger. The water we drink, the food we eat, the very air that we breathe are threatened with pollution. Our parks are overcrowded, our seashores overburdened. Green fields and dense forests are disappearing.

A few years ago we were greatly concerned about the "Ugly American." Today we must act to prevent an ugly America.

For once the battle is lost, once our natural splendor is destroyed, it can never be recaptured. And once man can no longer walk with beauty or wonder at nature, his spirit will wither and his sustenance[7] be wasted.

Part 4

A third place to build the Great Society is in the classrooms of America. There your children's lives will be shaped. Our society will not be great until every young mind is set free to scan the farthest reaches of thought and imagination. We are still far from that goal. Today, 8 million adult Americans, more than the entire population of Michigan, have not finished five years of school. Nearly 20 million have not finished eight years of school. Nearly 54 million—more than one-quarter of all America—have not even finished high school.

Each year more than 100,000 high school graduates, with proved ability, do not enter college because they cannot afford it. . . . Poverty must not be a bar to learning, and learning must offer an escape from poverty.

Part 5

These are three of the central issues of the Great Society. While our government has many programs directed at those issues, I do not pretend that we have the full answer to those problems. But I do promise this: We are going to assemble the best thought and the broadest knowledge from all over the world to find those answers for America.

For better or for worse, your generation has been appointed by history to deal with those problems and to lead America toward a new age. . . .

So, will you join in the battle to give every citizen the full equality which God enjoins and the law requires, whatever his belief, or race, or the color of his skin?

Will you join in the battle to give every citizen an escape from the crushing weight of poverty?

| Will you join in the battle to build the Great Society, to prove that our material[8] progress is only the foundation on which we will build a richer life of mind and spirit?

There are those timid souls that say this battle cannot be won; that we are condemned to a soulless wealth. I do not agree. We have the power to shape the civilization that we want. But we need your will and your labor and your hearts, if we are to build that kind of society. | |
| Those who came to this land sought to build more than just a new country. They sought a new world. So I have come here today to your campus to say that you can make their vision our reality. So let us from this moment begin our work so that in the future men will look back and say: It was then, after a long and weary way, that man turned the exploits[9] of his genius to the full enrichment of his life.

Thank you. Goodbye. | |

[1] indignation: anger about something that is unfair
[2] unbridled: unrestrained
[3] Aristotle: a famous philosopher
[4] ills: an evil or misfortune
[5] despoiling: ruining
[6] communion: a relationship with deep understanding
[7] sustenance: nourishment
[8] material: related to physical things
[9] exploits: heroic acts

Source: Lyndon Johnson. "The Great Society" speech. Delivered at the University of Michigan, Ann Arbor, May 22, 1964. Public domain.

Name: _____

Date: _____

1. Which statement from the speech best reveals its central idea?

    a. "The Great Society rests on abundance and liberty for all. It demands an end to poverty and racial injustice, to which we are totally committed in our time."

    b. "And our society will never be great until our cities are great."

    c. "Poverty must not be a bar to learning, and learning must offer an escape from poverty."

    d. "There are those timid souls that say this battle cannot be won; that we are condemned to a soulless wealth."

2. Explain why the answer you chose best reveals the central idea.

    _____

    _____

    _____

    _____

    _____

    _____

3. Reread the speech. How does each part develop the central idea?

	What is the supporting idea in this part of the speech?	How does this supporting idea develop the central idea of the speech?
Part 2		
Part 3		
Part 4		
Part 5		

4. Write a summary of the speech. Be sure to use what you know about the central idea and the gist of each part.

_____

_____

_____

_____

_____

5. Reread part 5. What opposing viewpoint does President Johnson acknowledge? How does he respond to it? Be sure to use what you know about the central idea and the gist of each part.

_____

_____

_____

_____

_____

6. Reread part 5 and think about the audience that is listening to this speech. How does each question that begins "Will you join in the battle" directly address the audience to whom Johnson is speaking?

_____

_____

_____

_____

7. Write a paragraph that answers the question: How is the central idea of the speech related to the central idea of "taking a stand"? Explain your answer, citing evidence from the text.

_____

_____

_____

_____

_____

_____

_____

_____

Story Impressions Note-Catcher

Name: _____

Date: _____

Directions: On your own, read the phrases from the novel quietly to yourself. Think about what this novel might be about:

- "I maintain that the Ewells started it all . . ."
- ". . . it really began with Andrew Jackson."
- "Maycomb was an old town . . ."
- "People moved slowly then."
- "Maycomb County had recently been told it had nothing to fear but fear itself."

Prereading Wonder: Based on the phrases and lines from the opening pages of the novel, what do you wonder about this novel?

_____

_____

_____

_____

_____

_____

_____

_____

_____

_____

_____

_____

_____

_____

EXPEDITIONARY
LEARNING

To Kill a Mockingbird Structured Notes Graphic Organizer

Chapter 1, Part A

Name: _____

Date: _____

What is the gist of what you read?

Focus Question

Based on what you have read so far, how would you describe Atticus? Be sure to use the best details from the novel in your answer.

Vocabulary

Word	Definition	Context clues: How did you figure out this word?
assuaged (3)		
"the disturbance" (4)		
ambled (5)		
vague optimism (6)		

To Kill a Mockingbird Structured Notes Graphic Organizer

Chapter 1, Part B

Name: _____

Date: _____

What is the gist of what you read?

Focus Question

Based on your reading of chapter 1, how do Jem, Scout, and Dill describe Boo Radley? Use the best evidence from the novel to support the description.

Vocabulary

Word	Definition	Context clues: How did you figure out this word?
satisfactory (6)		
routine contentment (8)		
malevolent phantom (8)		
stealthy (9)		
alien (9)		

To Kill a Mockingbird Structured Notes Graphic Organizer

Chapter 2

Name: _____

Date: _____

What is the gist of what you read?

Focus Question

Why does Scout stand up for Walter?

Vocabulary

Word	Definition	Context clues: How did you figure out this word?
meditating (17)		
illicitly (17)		
sentimentality (19)		
vexations (21)		
sojourn (22)		
Others:		

Atticus Note-Catcher

Name: _____

Date: _____

Atticus's words and actions	What do others say about Atticus?	Page	What does this reveal about Atticus's character?
"Atticus, the town lawyer, tries to do what is best for his clients, even if they don't listen to him."		4	Atticus has the best interest of others at heart. He tries to do the right thing no matter what.
"During his first five years in Maycomb, Atticus practiced economy more than anything; for several years thereafter he invested his earnings in his brother's education."		4	

EXPEDITIONARY
LEARNING

Word Strips

satisfactory

routine contentment

malevolent phantom

stealthy

alien

mediating

illicitly

vexations

sojourn

assuaged

ambled

vague optimism

Narrative Structure Graphic Organizer

Name: _____

Date: _____

Chapter: _____

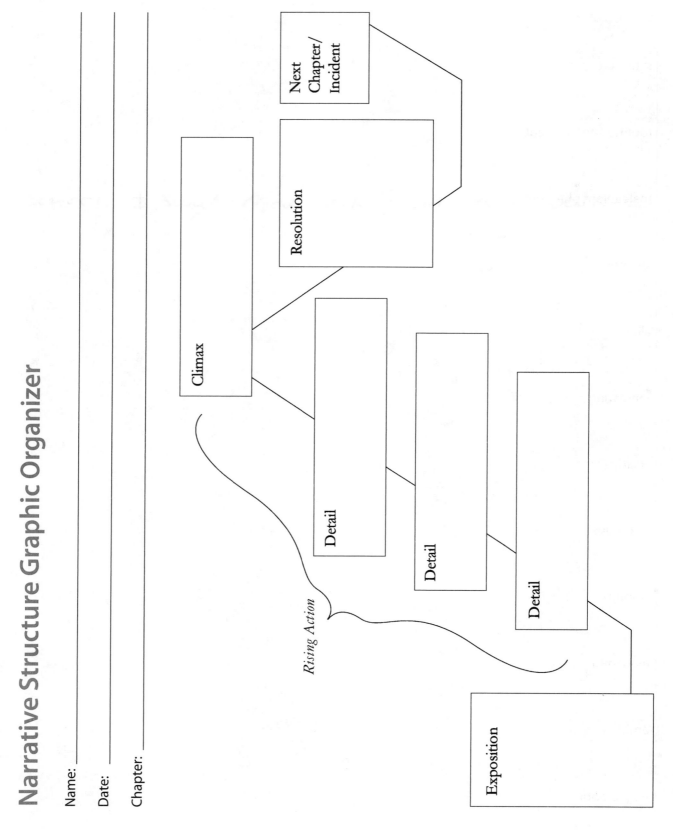

Next Chapter/Incident

Resolution

Climax

Detail

Detail

Detail

Rising Action

Exposition

Narrative Structure Note-Catcher

Name: _____

Date: _____

At the end of chapter 2, Scout's narration reflects on Miss Caroline by saying, "Had her conduct been more friendly toward me, I would have felt sorry for her."

Questions	Notes
1. Analyze the meaning of the chapter: What happened in the chapter to make Scout say this?	
2. How is the text structured? What is the job of each structural element of the text? (Use your Narrative Structure Graphic Organizer to help you answer this question.)	The job of the exposition in this chapter is . . . The job of the rising action in this chapter is . . . The job of the climax in this chapter is . . . The job of the resolution in this chapter is . . .
3. How does the structure of the chapter lead readers to understand what Scout means when she says, "Had her conduct been more friendly toward me, I would have felt sorry for her"?	

Summary Writing Homework

Name: _____

Date: _____

In chapter 2 of *To Kill a Mockingbird* . . .

chapter 2 is about scout being in
school & scout tried sticking up for walker
and ms caroline miss understood what
scout was trying to say about walter
being Poor

Vocabulary Square

Name: _____

Date: _____

Definition in Your Own Words	Synonym or Variations
Part of Speech and Prefix/Suffix/Root (as Applicable)	**Sketch or Symbol**

Text-Dependent Questions

Chapter 2 (Pages 19–22)

Name: _____

Date: _____

Text-Dependent Questions	Response Using the Strongest Evidence from the Text
1. Based on the text, what does the word *delegation* mean? Why might Lee describe the group of students as a *delegation*?	large group of people, she described them as a delegation because they will decide something.
2. Why is Scout the person who is chosen to explain things to Miss Caroline?	Scout has already talked to Miss Caroline that day "familiarity breeds understand"
3. Why does Lee include the information on Mr. Cunningham's dealings with Atticus in the middle of the classroom scene?	to provide background knowledge to the reader about Scouts knowledge of cunningham is.
4. Why does Miss Caroline say, "You're starting off on the wrong foot in every way, my dear"?	She has already been in trouble. Might be foreshadowing scout's behavior for rest of book.
5. What does Scout's stand reveal about her personality or character? Explain.	It shows that Scout is brave.

Exit Ticket

To Kill a Mockingbird, Chapter 2

Name: _____

Date: _____

1. Based on the scene reread in class, which word is closest in meaning to the word *mortification* (21)?

   a. Silliness

   b. Humiliation

   c. Hatred

   d. Seriousness

2. Atticus's statement that "Jem's definitions are very nearly accurate sometimes" (21) is meant to create which tone?

   a. Suspense

   b. Sentimentality

   c. Humor

   d. Seriousness

To Kill a Mockingbird Structured Notes Graphic Organizer

Chapter 3

Name: _michael J Padgett_

Date: _____

What is the gist of what you read?

Jem broke up a fight &
made things better

Focus Question

Who takes a stand and why? Explain using the strongest details from the novel.

Jem takes a stand because
one was bigger than the
other & he didnt wanna see
them fighting

Vocabulary

Word	Definition	Context clues: How did you figure out this word?
erratic (24)		
tranquility (24)		
contemptuous (27)		
compromise (31)		
concessions (31)		

Vocabulary Square

Name: _____

Date: _____

Definition in Your Own Words	Synonym or Variations
Part of Speech and Prefix/Suffix/Root (as Applicable)	**Sketch or Symbol**

Golden Rule Note-Catcher

Gallery Walk Quotes

Name: _____

Date: _____

The Golden Rule is a philosophy found in cultures and religions around the world. Pick your favorite from the Gallery Walk and write it in the following space:

_____

_____

In the following chart, identify what is the same and what is different about the various philosophies.

Same	Different

Put the idea of the Golden Rule in your own words:

_____

_____

The Golden Rule in *To Kill a Mockingbird* (RL.8.9):

Example in the novel (page no.)	Explain how this scene illustrates the Golden Rule.

Text-to-Film Comparison Note-Catcher

To Kill a Mockingbird, Part 1

Name: _____

Date: _____

Scene	What is the same? How does the film version stay faithful to the novel?	What is different? How does the film version depart from the novel?	Evaluation: Do the choices of the director or actor(s) effectively convey the central message of the text? Why or why not?
Read from "Something wrong, Scout?" (29) to "I never went to school" (32).			

EXPEDITIONARY
LEARNING

To Kill a Mockingbird Structured Notes Graphic Organizer

Chapter 4

Name: _____

Date: _____

What is the gist of what you read?

Focus Question

Atticus says, "You never really understand a person until you consider things from his point of view . . . until you climb into his skin and walk around in it" (chapter 3, p. 30). How is this advice taken or ignored in this chapter? Use the strongest evidence from the novel in your answer.

I read most of this & I couldn't understand it.

Vocabulary

Word	Definition	Context clues: How did you figure out this word?
auspicious (32)		
opposition (32)		
impulse (33)		
ethical (35)		
dreary (36)		
Others:		

Narrative Structure Chapter 4 Graphic Organizer

Name: _____

Date: _____

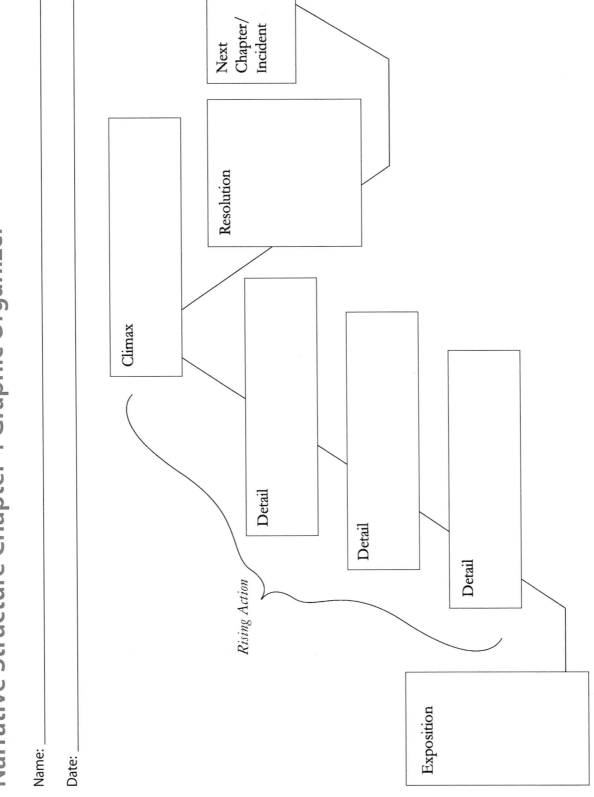

Next Chapter/Incident

Resolution

Climax

Detail

Detail

Detail

Rising Action

Exposition

Golden Rule in Karen Armstrong's TED Talk Note-Catcher

Name: _____

Date: _____

What does Karen Armstrong say is central to all the world's religions?

_____

_____

_____

_____

What is *compassion*?

_____

_____

_____

_____

According to Armstrong, how are compassion and the Golden Rule related?

_____

_____

_____

_____

What evidence from Armstrong's speech suggests that she might agree with Atticus's advice to Scout? "You never really understand a person until you consider things from his point of view . . . until you climb into his skin and walk around in it" (30).

_____

_____

_____

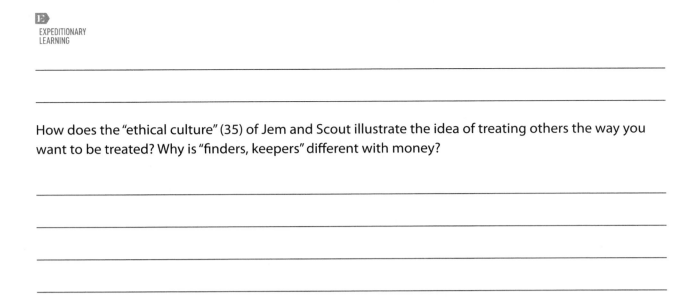

How does the "ethical culture" (35) of Jem and Scout illustrate the idea of treating others the way you want to be treated? Why is "finders, keepers" different with money?

_____

_____

_____

_____

EXPEDITIONARY
LEARNING

Networking Sessions Note-Catcher

Chapter 4

Name: _____

Date: _____

Why does Lee call it a "melancholy little drama" (39)?   _____ initials

_____

_____

_____

_____

What do the children actually "know" about the Radleys?   _____ initials

_____

_____

_____

_____

Are Jem, Scout, and Dill treating the Radleys with compassion? Explain.   _____ initials

_____

_____

_____

_____

To Kill a Mockingbird Structured Notes Graphic Organizer

Chapter 5

Name: _____

Date: _____

What is the gist of what you read?

Focus Question

Miss Maudie says, "Atticus Finch is the same in his house as he is in public" (46). What evidence so far proves this true?

Vocabulary

Word	Definition	Context clues: How did you figure out this word?
benign (42)		
tacit (42)		
cordiality (43)		
benevolence (43)		
morbid (43)		
edification (49)		

Vocabulary Strips

benign

tacit

cordiality

benevolence

morbid

edification

Vocabulary

Chapter 5

benign	adj.—good, kind, not dangerous
tacit	adj.—understood or implied without being said
cordiality	n.—kindness
benevolence	n.—generosity
morbid	adj.—related to disease or death; often thinking about gloomy things
edification	n.—spiritual, moral, or intellectual improvement.

To Kill a Mockingbird

Chapter 5 Text-Dependent Questions

Name: _____

Date: _____

1. Reread the middle of page 43. Why does Miss Maudie say Scout is being morbid?

    _____

    _____

    _____

    _____

2. Reread the top of page 44. What does "the best defense . . . was a spirited offense" mean?

    _____

    _____

    _____

    _____

3. Reread the middle of page 45. What does "The Bible in the hand of one man is worse than a whiskey bottle in the hand of . . . your father" mean?

    _____

    _____

    _____

    _____

4. Reread the top of page 46. What does Scout mean when she says, "Atticus don't ever do anything to Jem and me that he don't do in the yard"? How does this draw on the central idea of the Golden Rule?

_____

_____

_____

_____

EXPEDITIONARY
LEARNING

Quick Write

"Stop Tormenting That Man!"

Name: _____

Date: _____

Do a Quick Write to address the prompt:

"I'm going to tell you something and tell you one time: stop tormenting that man" (49). What does this statement show about Atticus's belief in the Golden Rule?

_____

_____

_____

_____

_____

_____

_____

_____

_____

_____

_____

_____

_____

_____

_____

_____

_____

To Kill a Mockingbird Structured Notes Graphic Organizer

Chapters 6 and 7

Name: _____

Date: _____

What is the gist of what you read?

Focus Question

What does the reader learn about Jem, Scout, and Boo in these chapters? Use the strongest evidence from the novel in your answer.

EXPEDITIONARY
LEARNING

Vocabulary

Word	Definition	Context clues: How did you figure out this word?
commotion (54)		
malignant (55)		
pilgrimage (57)		
burdensome (61)		
rendered (61)		

Narrative Structure Chapter 6 Graphic Organizer

Name:

Date:

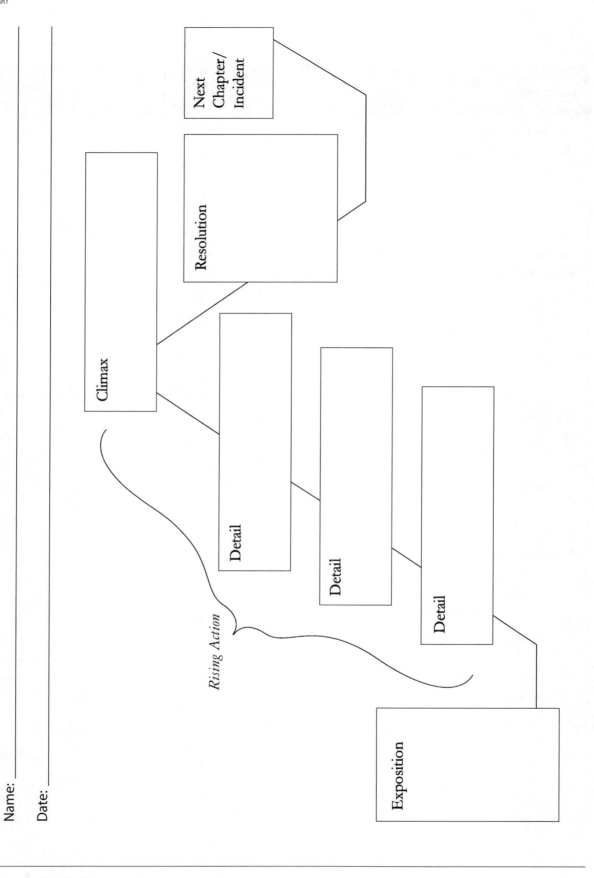

EXPEDITIONARY
LEARNING

"Those Winter Sundays"

By Robert Hayden

Source: "Those Winter Sundays." Copyright © 1966 by Robert Hayden. Robert Hayden, Collected Poems of Robert Hayden, edited by Frederick Glaysher (New York: Liveright Pubishing, 1966). Used by permission of Liveright Publishing Corporation.

Sundays too my father got up early
and put his clothes on in the blueblack cold,
then with cracked hands that ached
from labor in the weekday weather made
banked fires blaze. No one ever thanked him.

I'd wake and hear the cold splintering, breaking.
When the rooms were warm, he'd call,
and slowly I would rise and dress,
fearing the chronic angers of that house,

Speaking indifferently to him,
who had driven out the cold
and polished my good shoes as well.
What did I know, what did I know
of love's austere and lonely offices?

"Those Winter Sundays"

Close Reading Note-Catcher

Name: _____

Date: _____

1. What do you think the gist of the poem might be?

_____

_____

2. Vocabulary Chart

Word	Predicted meaning from context	Actual meaning
banked (line 5)		
chronic (line 9)		
indifferently (line 10)		
austere (line 14)		
offices (line 14)		

3. Draw the images in three stanzas as thoroughly and with as much detail as you can. Go back to the poem as much as you need to as you draw. *Hint: Be careful with the third stanza. Notice this box for the third stanza has two parts. Pay attention to that in your drawing.*

Stanza 1	Stanza 2	Stanza 3
Lines 1–5	Lines 6–9	Lines 10–12
		Lines 13–14

4. What do these stanzas tell us about the narrator and his father? What do they care about?

Evidence about the father: What does he do in the poem?	Elaborate/analyze/infer: What does this show about what the father cares about?

Evidence about the narrator: What does he do in the poem?	Elaborate/analyze/infer: What does this show about what the narrator cares about?

5. In the last two lines of the poem, the poet tells us how he feels about his relationship with his father. How does the poet structure this poem so that the last two lines accomplish this?

    The poet structures his poem so that the last two lines explain how he feels about his relationship with his father. He realizes that, when he was young, he didn't understand how much his father loved him, and he regrets this.

In the first stanza,

_____

_____

_____

In the second stanza,

_____

_____

_____

In the first three lines of the third stanza,

_____

_____

_____

In the last two lines of the third stanza,

_____

_____

_____

6. What do you think this poem seems to be saying about the Golden Rule?

Discuss briefly with a peer, capture your ideas, and then you'll come to a consensus about this with your class.

Notes

Class Consensus

Comparing and Contrasting Text Structures

	"Those Winter Sundays"	Chapter 6
How does this text relate to the Golden Rule?		
How is this text structured?		
How does the structure help create the meaning?		

EXPEDITIONARY
LEARNING

To Kill a Mockingbird Structured Notes Graphic Organizer

Chapter 8

Name: _____

Date: _____

What is the gist of what you read?

Focus Question

What is an example of the Golden Rule in this chapter? Use the strongest evidence from the novel in your answer.

EXPEDITIONARY
LEARNING

Vocabulary

Word	Definition	Context clues: How did you figure out this word?
unfathomable (63)		
aberration (63)		
procured (66)		
caricature (67)		
quelled (71)		

"Incident"

By Countee Cullen

(For Eric Walrond)

Source: Copyrights held by the Amistad Research Center Tulane University, administrated by Thompson and Thompson, Brooklyn, New York.

Once riding in old Baltimore,
Heart-filled, head-filled with glee,
I saw a Baltimorean
Keep looking straight at me.

Now I was eight and very small,
And he was no whit bigger,
And so I smiled, but he poked out
His tongue, and called me, "Nigger."

I saw the whole of Baltimore
From May until December;
Of all the things that happened there
That's all that I remember.

What does not fit	Identify the Juxtapos	Purpose
Poked out his tongue	how they towards one another "I Smiled & he poked out his tongue"	Shows the impact actions towards each other has.

How does it illustrate the golden rule?

Shows what happens when we don't follow the "golden rule"

"Incident"

Structure Note-Catcher

Name: _____

Date: _____

1. What do you think the gist of the poem might be?

_____

_____

2. What do the three stanzas tell us about the narrator and his experience in Baltimore?

Evidence from stanza 1	Elaborate/analyze/infer: What does this show about the narrator?

Evidence from stanza 2	Elaborate/analyze/infer: What does this show about the narrator?

Evidence from stanza 3	Elaborate/analyze/infer: What does this show about the narrator?

3. In the last two lines of the poem, the poet reflects back on his time in Baltimore. How does the poet structure this poem so that the last two lines accomplish this?

Focus statement: The poet structures his poem so that the last two lines show how important that experience was.

In the first stanza,

_____

_____

_____

Then in the second stanza,

_____

_____

_____

In the first two lines of the third stanza,

_____

_____

_____

By the last two lines of the third stanza,

_____

_____

_____

4. What do you think this poem seems to be saying about the Golden Rule? Discuss briefly with a peer, capture your ideas, and then you'll come to a consensus about this with your class.

    Notes:

_____

_____

_____

_____

_____

_____

_____

_____

Class consensus:

_____

_____

_____

_____

_____

_____

_____

Analyzing Scout's Perspective about Boo Radley Note-Catcher

Name: _____

Date: _____

Chapter	Scout's Perspective	Evidence
1		
4		
6 and 7		
8		

Jigsaw Excerpts

Chapter 1

"Inside the house lived a malevolent phantom. People said he existed, but Jem and I had never seen him" (9).

"Jem gave a reasonable description of Boo: Boo was about six and a half feet tall, judging from his tracks; he dined on raw squirrels and any cats he could catch. That's why his hands were bloodstained—if you ate an animal raw, you could never wash the blood off. There was a long jagged scar that ran across his face; what teeth he had were yellow and rotten; his eyes popped, and he drooled most of the time" (13).

Jigsaw Excerpts

Chapter 4

Two live oaks stood at the edge of the Radley lot; their roots reached out into the side-road and made it bumpy. Something about one of the trees attracted my attention.

Some tinfoil was sticking in a knot-hole just above my eye level, winking at me in the afternoon sun. I stood on tiptoe, hastily looked around once more, reached into the hole, and withdrew two pieces of chewing gum minus their outer wrappers.

My first impulse was to get it into my mouth as quickly as possible, but I remembered where I was. I ran home, and on our front porch I examined my loot. The gum looked fresh. I sniffed it and it smelled all right. I licked it and waited for a while. When I did not die I crammed it into my mouth: Wrigley's Double-Mint.

When Jem came home he asked me where I got such a wad. I told him I found it.

"Don't eat things you find, Scout."

"This wasn't on the ground, it was in a tree."

Jem growled.

"Well it was," I said. "It was sticking in that tree yonder, the one comin' from school."

"Spit it out right now!"

I spat it out. The tang was fading, anyway. "I've been chewin' it all afternoon and I ain't dead yet, not even sick." (33)

Jigsaw Excerpts

Chapters 6 and 7

"Had Jem's pants been safely on him, we would not have slept much anyway. Every night-sound I heard from my cot on the back porch was magnified three-fold; every scratch of feet on gravel was Boo Radley seeking revenge, every passing Negro laughing in the night was Boo Radley loose and after us; insects splashing against the screen were Boo Radley's insane fingers picking the wire to pieces; the chinaberry trees were malignant, hovering, alive" (55).

One afternoon when we were crossing the schoolyard toward home, Jem suddenly said: "There's something I didn't tell you."

As this was his first complete sentence in several days, I encouraged him: "About what?"

"About that night."

"You've never told me anything about that night," I said.

Jem waved my words away as if fanning gnats. He was silent for a while, then he said, "When I went back for my breeches—they were all in a tangle when I was gettin' out of 'em, I couldn't get 'em loose. When I went back—" Jem took a deep breath. "When I went back, they were folded across the fence . . . like they were expectin' me."

"Across—"

"And something else—" Jem's voice was flat. "Show you when we get home. They'd been sewed up. Not like a lady sewed 'em, like somethin' I'd try to do. All crooked. It's almost like—"

"—somebody knew you were comin' back for 'em" (58).

Jigsaw Excerpts

Chapter 8

It was obvious that he had not followed a word Jem said, for all Atticus said was, "You're right. We'd better keep this and the blanket to ourselves. Someday, maybe, Scout can thank him for covering her up."

"Thank who?" I asked.

"Boo Radley. You were so busy looking at the fire you didn't know it when he put the blanket around you."

My stomach turned to water and I nearly threw up when Jem held out the blanket and crept toward me. "He sneaked out of the house—turn 'round—sneaked up, an' went like this!"

Atticus said dryly, "Do not let this inspire you to further glory, Jeremy."

Jem scowled, "I ain't gonna do anything to him," but I watched the spark of fresh adventure leave his eyes. "Just think, Scout," he said, "if you'd just turned around, you'da seen him" (72).

To Kill a Mockingbird Structured Notes Graphic Organizer

Chapter 9

Name: _____

Date: _____

What is the gist of what you read?

Focus Question

Atticus says, "Simply because we were licked a hundred years before we started is no reason for us not to try to win" (76). What does he mean? Explain the significance of this statement. Use the strongest evidence from the novel in your answer.

Vocabulary

Word	Definition	Context clues: How did you figure out this word?
inordinately (76)		
ingenious (77)		
wary (78)		
innate (78)		
obstreperous (85)		
"Maycomb's usual disease" (88)		

Narrative Structure Chapter 8 Graphic Organizer

Name: _____

Date: _____

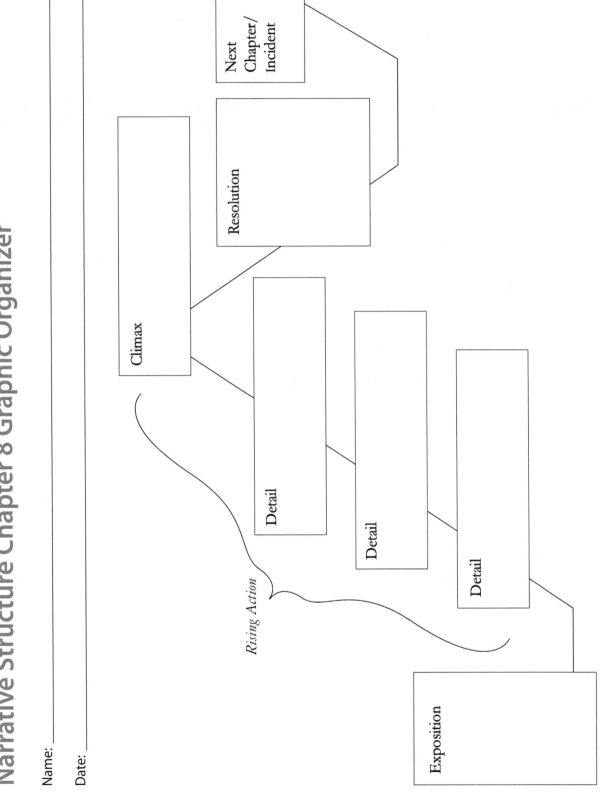

Comparing and Contrasting Text Structures

Name: _____

Date: _____

	"Incident"	Chapter 8
How does this text relate to the Golden Rule?		
How is this text structured?		
How does the structure help create the meaning?		

EXPEDITIONARY
LEARNING

Text-to-Film Comparison Note-Catcher

Chapter 9 text	What's the same? How does the film version stay faithful to the novel?	What's different? How does the film version depart from the novel?	Evaluation: Do the choices of the director or actor(s) effectively convey the central message of the text? Why or why not?
Paragraphs 1–5 "Do you defend niggers, Atticus?" to ". . . why do you send me to school?"			
Paragraph 6 "My father looked at me mildly."			
Paragraphs 7–10 "But I was worrying another bone." to "John Taylor was nice enough to give us a postponement."			

Chapter 9 text	What's the same? How does the film version stay faithful to the novel?	What's different? How does the film version depart from the novel?	Evaluation: Do the choices of the director or actor(s) effectively convey the central message of the text? Why or why not?
Paragraphs 11–15 "If you shouldn't be defendin' him . . ." to "Why?"			
Paragraph 16 "Because I could never . . ."			
Paragraph 17–20 "Atticus, are we going to win it?" to "'Simply because we were licked a hundred years before we started is no reason for us not to try to win,' Atticus said."			

Written Conversation Note-Catcher

Reread pages 87–91. Scout, as the narrator, ends the chapter by saying: "It was not until many years later that I realized he (Atticus) wanted me to hear every word he said."

Why might Atticus want her to hear every word? What makes you think as you do?

I Say	My Peer Responds	I Build	My Peer Concludes

To Kill a Mockingbird Structured Notes Graphic Organizer

Chapter 10

Name: _____

Date: _____

What is the gist of what you read?

Focus Question

Atticus says, "Remember it's a sin to kill a mockingbird." Put this statement in your own words. What does Atticus really mean? Use the strongest evidence from the novel in your answer.

Vocabulary

Word	Definition	Context clues: How did you figure out this word?
feeble (89)		
inconspicuous (89)		
attributes (89)		
peril (91)		
vaguely articulate (97)		

EXPEDITIONARY
LEARNING

Chapter 10 Note-Catcher

Name: _____

Date: _____

Round 1	Round 2
What does *feeble* mean?	What does "it's a sin to kill a mockingbird" mean?
Why do Scout and Jem think that Atticus is feeble?	How do you think it relates to the title?

Round 3	Round 4
What does Miss Maudie mean when she says, "People in their right minds never take pride in their talents"?	Based on the last three rounds, what do you learn about Atticus in this chapter?
	How does this chapter relate to Atticus taking a stand for Tom Robinson?

EXPEDITIONARY
LEARNING

Exit Ticket

Name: _____

Date: _____

1. How do the events in chapter 10 relate to the Golden Rule?

    a. They show that not everyone needs to be good at the same things.

    b. It's important to treat everyone with kindness and respect because you never know all there is to know about a person.

    c. Animals and people should be treated equally.

    d. Elderly people deserve respect.

2. Use the best evidence to support your answer:

To Kill a Mockingbird Structured Notes Graphic Organizer

Chapter 11

What is the gist of what you read?

Focus Question

How is the Golden Rule illustrated in chapter 11? Use the strongest evidence from the novel in your answer.

EXPEDITIONARY
LEARNING

Vocabulary

Word	Definition	Context clues: How did you figure out this word?
confined (99)		
livid (100)		
commence (106)		
undulate (107)		
beholden (111)		

EXPEDITIONARY
LEARNING

End-of-Unit 1 Assessment: Analyzing Author's Craft in *To Kill a Mockingbird*

Allusion, Text Structure, Connections to Traditional Themes, and Figurative Language

Name: _____

Date: _____

Part A. Author's Craft: Text Structure and Connecting the Novel to Traditional Themes Like the Golden Rule

Use the Narrative Structure organizer to show the narrative structure of chapter 11.

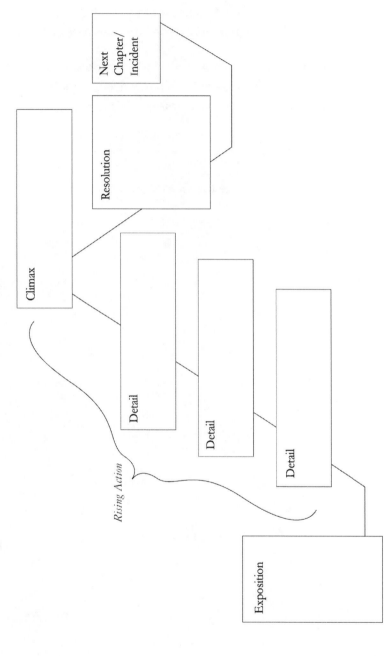

Read the following excerpt from chapter 11 of *To Kill a Mockingbird* and explain how it illustrates the Golden Rule:

_____

"Easy does it, son," Atticus would say. "She's an old lady and she's ill. You just hold your head high and be a gentleman. Whatever she says to you, it's your job not to let her make you mad."

Jem would say she must not be very sick, she hollered so. When the three of us came to her house, Atticus would sweep off his hat, wave gallantly to her and say, "Good evening, Mrs. Dubose! You look like a picture this evening" (100).

_____

How does this illustrate the Golden Rule?

Read the poem and answer the questions that follow.

Solitude

By Ella Wheeler Wilcox

Source: First published in the February 25, 1883, issue of the New York Sun. Public domain.

Laugh, and the world laughs with you;

Weep, and you weep alone.

For the sad old earth must borrow its mirth,

But has trouble enough of its own.

Sing, and the hills will answer;

Sigh, it is lost on the air.

The echoes bound to a joyful sound,

But shrink from voicing care.

Rejoice, and men will seek you;

Grieve, and they turn and go.

They want full measure of all your pleasure,

But they do not need your woe.

Be glad, and your friends are many;

Be sad, and you lose them all.

There are none to decline your nectared wine,

But alone you must drink life's gall.

Feast, and your halls are crowded;

Fast, and the world goes by.

Succeed and give, and it helps you live,

But no man can help you die.

There is room in the halls of pleasure

For a long and lordly train,

But one by one we must all file on

Through the narrow aisles of pain.

mirth: laughter, happiness

solitude: loneliness, alone

gall: bile

fast: not eat

train: group of friends

1. What is the poem mostly about?

    a. Laughter is the answer to a happy life.

    b. What you put out, the world returns to you.

    c. Positive actions result in positive returns.

    d. Negative actions result in negative returns.

2. What do the first two stanzas tell us about what the narrator has learned about life?

Evidence from Stanza 1	Elaborate/analyze/infer: What does this show about the narrator?

Evidence from Stanza 2	Elaborate/analyze/infer: What does this show about the narrator?

3. In the last stanza of the poem, the poet sums up what she has learned about living, dying, and the support of others. How does the poet structure this poem so that the last stanza reveals these lessons? Use the organizer that follows to explain your answer.

In stanzas 1 and 2,

_____

_____

_____

_____

By the last stanza of the poem,

_____

_____

_____

_____

4.   What do you think this poem seems to be saying about the Golden Rule?

_____

_____

_____

_____

	"Solitude"	Chapter 11
How does this text relate to the Golden Rule?		
How is this text structured?		
How does the structure affect the meaning?		

EXPEDITIONARY
LEARNING

Part B. Author's Craft: Allusion

In chapter 11, Jem reads *Ivanhoe* by Sir Walter Scott aloud to Mrs. Dubose. *Ivanhoe* was published in 1820. It takes place in England in the same time period as King Richard and Robin Hood. The central idea of *Ivanhoe* is reconciliation, the act of bringing people together again.

Reread the following passage, then analyze this allusion's impact on the meaning of chapter 11.

The following Monday afternoon Jem and I climbed the steep front steps to Mrs. Dubose's house and padded down the open hallway. Jem, armed with *Ivanhoe* and full of superior knowledge, knocked at the second door on the left.

"Mrs. Dubose?" he called.

Jessie opened the wood door and unlatched the screen door.

"Is that you, Jem Finch?" she said. "You got your sister with you. I don't know—"

"Let 'em both in, Jessie," said Mrs. Dubose. Jessie admitted us and went off to the kitchen.

An oppressive odor met us when we crossed the threshold, an odor I had met many times in rain-rotted gray houses where there are coal-oil lamps, water dippers, and unbleached domestic sheets. It always made me afraid, expectant, watchful.

In the corner of the room was a brass bed, and in the bed was Mrs. Dubose. I wondered if Jem's activities had put her there, and for a moment I felt sorry for her. She was lying under a pile of quilts and looked almost friendly.

There was a marble-topped washstand by her bed; on it were a glass with a teaspoon in it, a red ear syringe, a box of absorbent cotton, and a steel alarm clock standing on three tiny legs.

"So you brought that dirty little sister of yours, did you?" was her greeting.

Jem said quietly, "My sister ain't dirty and I ain't scared of you," although I noticed his knees shaking.

I was expecting a tirade, but all she said was, "You may commence reading, Jeremy."

Jem sat down in a cane-bottom chair and opened *Ivanhoe*. I pulled up another one and sat beside him.

"Come closer," said Mrs. Dubose. "Come to the side of the bed."

We moved our chairs forward. This was the nearest I had ever been to her, and the thing I wanted most to do was move my chair back again (105–106).

1. What impact does the allusion to *Ivanhoe* have on the meaning of chapter 11?

    a. It emphasizes that Jem wants revenge on Mrs. Dubose.

    b. It shows that Jem loves adventure novels.

    c. It makes Jem and Scout's relationship clearer.

    d. It shows that this chapter brings Jem and Mrs. Dubose together peacefully.

    e. It brings up the idea of slavery.

    f. It refers to the court system.

    g. It makes Mrs. Dubose look even meaner.

2. Justify your answer using evidence from the text.

_____

_____

_____

_____

_____

_____

_____

_____

_____

_____

_____

_____

_____

_____

_____

_____

_____

_____

Part C. Author's Craft: Figurative Language

1. What is the figurative meaning of the underlined phrase? "The day after Jem's twelfth birthday <u>his money was burning up his pockets</u>, so we headed for town in the early afternoon. Jem thought he had enough to buy a miniature steam engine for himself and a twirling baton for me" (100).

   a. The coins in Jem's pockets were hot because of the sun.

   b. Jem was eager to spend his birthday money.

   c. Jem felt guilty about having money in his pockets.

   d. Jem had stolen the money in his pockets.

To Kill a Mockingbird Structured Notes Graphic Organizer

Chapters 12 and 13

Chapter 12 Summary

As summer begins, Scout is crushed to discover that Dill will not be joining them. When Atticus has to go out of town for two weeks, Calpurnia decides that she will take them to church with her. Aside from one woman, Jem and Scout are welcomed into the African church with open arms, and they're amazed to see how different it is from their own staid church service.

They're also amazed to find out that the church collection is going to Helen Robinson, Tom's wife, and the Reverend is not letting anyone leave until they've collected $10, which is what she needs each week to support her kids. Purses are scraped and pockets searched, and finally everyone comes up with enough money and the doors are opened. They also find out that Tom is in jail because he's accused of raping Bob Ewell's daughter, Mayella (who is white), which is why the entire town is in an uproar over Atticus taking on the case. When they get back home from church, they find Aunt Alexandra on the front porch swing waiting for them.

What is the gist of what you read?

Focus Question

What is an example of the Golden Rule in this chapter? Use the strongest evidence from the novel in your answer.

Vocabulary

Word	Definition	Context clues: How did you figure out this word?
appalling (115)		
diligently (116)		
contentious (119)		
tactful (128)		
caste system (131)		
prerogative (129)		

Three Threes in a Row Note-Catcher

Who takes a stand in chapter 11? Explain.	On page 105, Atticus says, "Before I can live with other folks, I've got to live with myself. The one thing that doesn't abide by majority rule is a person's conscience." What does this quote reveal about Atticus's character? How does this relate to the Golden Rule?	On page 128, Atticus says, "The summer's going to be a hot one." Explain what this means.
Why does Atticus refer to Mrs. Dubose as "the bravest person I ever knew"?	On page 112, Atticus says, "I wanted you to see what real courage is, instead of getting the idea that courage is a man with a gun in his hand. It's when you know you're licked before you begin but you begin anyway and you see it through no matter what. You rarely win, but sometimes you do." What does this quote reveal about Atticus's character? How does this relate to the Golden Rule?	Scout recalls about Aunt Alexandra, "She never let a chance escape her to point out the shortcomings of other tribal groups to the greater glory of our own" (129). Explain what this means.

Why does Aunt Alexandra think the Finches are special?	On page 108, Atticus says, "I do my best to love everybody . . . I'm hard put, sometimes." What does this quote reveal about Atticus's character? How does this relate to the Golden Rule?	On page 127, Lee writes, "Aunt Alexandra's visits from the Landing were rare, and she traveled in state." Explain what this means.

To Kill a Mockingbird Structured Notes Graphic Organizer

Chapters 14 and 15

Name: _____

Date: _____

Chapter 14 Summary

As life continues with Aunty in the house, one night Scout goes to bed and steps on something soft and warm and round, which she thinks is a snake. After calling Jem in for a thorough investigation underneath her bed, they find Dill under there, dirty and starving and still his same old self. Scout finds out the reason Dill ran off was because his parents just aren't interested in him, and he spends most of his days alone. He spends the night with them, uncertain what the next day will bring.

What is the gist of what you read in chapter 15?

Focus Question

In chapter 15, who takes a stand? Why? Use the strongest evidence from the novel in your answer.

Vocabulary

Word	Definition	Context clues: How did you figure out this word?
antagonize (137)		
infallible (140)		
ominous (146)		
acquiescence (154)		
impassive (154)		

EXPEDITIONARY
LEARNING

Analyzing Scout's and the Reader's Perspectives Note-Catcher

Name: _____

Date: _____

Excerpt	Scout's Perspective: What does Scout think is happening?	Reader's Perspective: What does the reader understand is happening?
"'Do you really think so?' This was the second time I heard Atticus ask that question in two days, and it meant somebody's man would get jumped. This was too good to miss. I broke away from Jem and ran as fast as I could to Atticus" (152).		
"I sought once more for a familiar face, and at the center of the semicircle I found one. 'Hey, Mr. Cunningham.' The man did not hear me, it seemed. 'Hey, Mr. Cunningham. How's your entailment gettin' along?'" (153).		

'"Entailments are bad,' I was advising him, when I slowly awoke to the fact that I was addressing the entire aggregation. The men were all looking at me, some had their mouths half-open. Atticus had stopped poking at Jem: they were standing together beside Dill. Their attention amounted to fascination. Atticus's mouth, even, was half-open, an attitude he had once described as uncouth. Our eyes met and he shut it" (154).		
"I looked around and up at Mr. Cunningham, whose face was equally impassive. Then he did a peculiar thing. He squatted down and took me by both shoulders. 'I'll tell him you said hey, little lady,' he said. Then he straightened up and waved a big paw. 'Let's clear out,' he called. 'Let's get going, boys'" (154).		

What effect does Scout's misunderstanding create for the reader?

a.   It increases the tension in a suspenseful scene.

b.   It causes the reader to doubt the intentions of the group of men who have arrived at the jailhouse.

c.   It relieves the tension in an otherwise serious scene.

d.   It creates a feeling of confusion around Atticus playing checkers at night in front of the jailhouse.

Text-to-Film Comparison Note-Catcher

Taking a Stand at the Jailhouse

Name: _____

Date: _____

Chapter 15 text pages 151–155	What's the same? How does the film version stay faithful to the novel?	What's different? How does the film version depart from the novel?	Evaluation: Do the choices of the director or actors effectively convey the central message of the text? Why or why not?
151–152			
153–154			
155			

Pick one choice of the director or actors in this scene. Does it effectively convey the central message of the text? Why or why not?

| |
| |
| |

To Kill a Mockingbird Structured Notes Graphic Organizer

Chapters 16 and 17

Name: _____

Date: _____

Chapter 16 Summary (155–162)

The next morning, Saturday, the whole county begins to file into town to watch Tom Robinson's trial. Jem and Scout provide a constant commentary for Dill, explaining the background and tendencies of everyone who passes. After lunch, they head into town themselves to watch the trial.

What is the gist of the end of chapter 16 and of chapter 17?

Focus Question

On page 163, Scout learns that her father was appointed to defend Tom Robinson. She observes, "The court appointed Atticus to defend him. Atticus aimed to defend him. That's what they didn't like about it. It was confusing." What does the reader understand about why the townspeople are upset that Scout doesn't? Use the strongest evidence from the novel in your answer.

Vocabulary

Word	Definition	Context clues: How did you figure out this word?
formidable (159)		
amiably (169)		
acrimonious (171)		
benignly (172)		
genially (175)		

Analyzing Themes Note-Catcher

Directions: With your Discussion Appointment peer, choose the strongest evidence from the novel to answer the following questions.

Part A. The Golden Rule

1. What does Atticus mean when he says, "You children last night made Walter Cunningham stand in my shoes for a minute. That was enough" (157)?	
2. What does Walter Cunningham understand about Atticus when he "stood in his shoes"?	
3. How does this quote relate to what Atticus says earlier in the novel: "You never really understand a person until you consider things from his point of view—until you climb into his skin and walk around in it" (30)?	
4. How do these two quotes relate to the Golden Rule?	

Part B. Taking a Stand

	Atticus	Mr. Cunningham
1. What is each character taking a stand about?		
2. How does each character take a stand?		
3. How does Mr. Cunningham's stand change after he "stood" in Atticus's shoes?		

Exit Ticket

Directions: With your Discussion Appointment peer, choose the strongest evidence from the novel to answer the following questions.

How is each central idea or theme demonstrated in today's lesson? Use the strongest details from the novel to support your answer. You may use the Analyzing Themes Note-Catcher.	
The Golden Rule	
Taking a stand	
What is the connection between the two central ideas of the Golden Rule and taking a stand?	

To Kill a Mockingbird Structured Notes Graphic Organizer

Chapter 18

Name: _____

Date: _____

What is the gist of what you read?

Focus Question

Why do you think Atticus speaks so formally to Mayella during her testimony? What is your impression of Atticus based on Lee's descriptions during Mayella's testimony? Use the strongest evidence from the novel to explain your answer.

Vocabulary

Word	Definition	Context clues: How did you figure out this word?
mollified (180)		
arid (185)		
wrathfully (185)		

Mid-Unit Assessment

Text-to-Film and Perspective Comparison of *To Kill a Mockingbird*

Name: _____

Date: _____

Part A. Summarizing Narrative Text

1. In the space that follows, write a summary of chapter 18 that follows the narrative structure. Be sure to include the exposition, rising action, climax, falling action, and resolution.

Part B. Analyzing Point of View

2a. On page 188, Lee writes, "Somehow, Atticus had hit her hard in a way that was not clear to me, but it gave him no pleasure to do so." What does the phrase "hit her hard" mean in this context? Support your answer with two details from the text.

2b. Thinking about the quote in the previous question, what does the reader understand about Atticus's questions that Scout does not?

    a. Atticus's questions hurt Mayella's feelings.

    b. Atticus's questions prove that Tom is guilty.

    c. Atticus's questions prove that Mayella's testimony is unreliable.

    d. Atticus's questions prove that Bob Ewell committed the crime.

2c. What effect does Scout's description of Atticus's questions create for the reader?

    a. Doubt that Mayella was attacked by Tom Robinson

    b. Sadness that Mayella doesn't have any friends

    c. Joy that Atticus is winning

    d. Surprise that Scout remains in the courtroom

Part C. Text-to-Film Comparison

After viewing the courtroom scene from the film, analyze the extent to which the film stays faithful to the text.

Chapter 18: Reread from "We've had a good visit, Miss Mayella, and now I guess we'd better get to the case" (184) to "It most certainly is" (187).	What's the same? How does the film version stay faithful to the novel?	What's different? How does the film version depart from the novel?	Evaluation: Do the choices of the director or actor(s) effectively convey the central message of the text? Why or why not?

Pick either the director or actors in this scene. Does the scene effectively convey the central message of the text? Why or why not?

EXPEDITIONARY
LEARNING

To Kill a Mockingbird Structured Notes Graphic Organizer

Chapter 19

Name: _____

Date: _____

What is the gist of what you read?

Focus Question

What is the difference between Atticus's cross-examination of Mayella in chapter 18 and Mr. Gilmer's cross-examination of Tom in chapter 19? Why do you think the author wants us to see both of these cross-examinations? Use the strongest evidence to explain your answer.

Vocabulary

Word	Definition	Context clues: How did you figure out this word?
volition (192)		
subtlety (195)		
expunge (196)		
candid (198)		
impudent (198)		

EXPEDITIONARY
LEARNING

Vocabulary Square

Definition in your own words	Synonyms or variations
Part of speech and prefix/suffix/root (as applicable)	**Sketch or symbol**

Atticus Cross-Examination Note-Catcher

Chapter 18 questions	Answer supported with the strongest evidence from the novel	How does Mr. Gilmer compare? (to be completed in outside circle)
Which words or phrases does Atticus use to address Mayella when he speaks to her?		
Considering the words and phrases you wrote above, how would you best describe how Atticus treats Mayella?		

Debrief Fishbowl: What is the difference between Atticus and Mr. Gilmer? How do the differences help you understand Atticus's character? What connections can you draw to the Golden Rule?

Chapter 18 questions	Answer supported with the strongest evidence from the novel	How does Atticus compare? (to be completed in outside circle)
What words or phrases does Mr. Gilmer use to address Tom when he speaks to him?		
Considering the words and phrases you wrote above, how would you best describe how Mr. Gilmer treated Tom?		

Debrief Fishbowl: What is the difference between Atticus and Mr. Gilmer? How do the differences help you understand Atticus's character? What connections can you draw to the Golden Rule?

To Kill a Mockingbird Structured Notes Graphic Organizer

Chapters 20 and 21

Name: _____

Date: _____

What is the gist of what you read?

Focus Question

Mr. Raymond says, "Miss Jean Louise, you don't know your pa's not a run-of-the-mill man, it'll take a few years for that to sink in—you haven't seen enough of the world yet. You haven't seen this town, but all you gotta do is step back inside the courthouse" (201). What does Mr. Raymond mean? Explain using the strongest evidence from the novel to support your answer.

Vocabulary

Word	Definition	Context clues: How did you figure out this word?
detachment (202)		
subsequent (203)		
unmitigated (204)		
temerity (204)		
integrity (205)		
acquit (207)		
indignant (207)		

Irony Example

After spending hours putting a bike together, Dad said, "Easy as 1, 2, 3."

Literal and Figurative Meanings	
1. How was putting the bike together literally as easy as 1, 2, 3?	2. How was putting the bike together figuratively as easy as 1, 2, 3?
The dad could have said this literally because there actually may have been three steps.	*He also could have meant this figuratively because counting to three is easy, so this simile is a way of saying "easy."*
Describe the irony of Dad's statement. **Irony: words that express something different from and often opposite to their literal meaning.**	
3. What do Dad's words mean <u>without</u> irony?	4. Dad is speaking <u>with</u> irony here. What do his words really mean?
Without irony, Dad's words mean that it was an easy job with three steps.	*Dad's words really mean that it was not an easy job at all, since it took him four hours to do just three steps.*

EXPEDITIONARY
LEARNING

Atticus's Closing Speech Note-Catcher

Part A. Word Choice: Analyzing Meaning and Irony

"This case is as simple as black and white."

Literal and Figurative Meanings	
1. How is this case literally about black and white?	2. How is this case black and white, figuratively speaking?

Describe the irony of Atticus's statement.	
Irony: words that express something different from and often opposite to their literal meaning.	
3. What do Atticus's words mean without irony?	4. Atticus is speaking with irony here. What do his words really mean?

Part B. Taking a Stand in the Courtroom

After Atticus's speech to the court in chapter 21, how do both the jury and the black community take a stand? How is this tied to the Golden Rule? Explain.

To Kill a Mockingbird Structured Notes Graphic Organizer

Chapters 22 and 23

Name: _____

Date: _____

What is the gist of what you read?

Focus Question

Miss Maudie says, "There are some men in this world who were born to do our unpleasant jobs for us. Your father's one of them" (215). What does she mean? What evidence from the novel supports this statement?

Vocabulary

Word	Definition	Context clues: How did you figure out this word?
cynical (214)		
fatalistic (215)		
ruefully (215)		
wryly (218)		
furtive (218)		
commutes (219)		
vehement (221)		

Vocabulary Square

Name: _____

Date: _____

Definition in your own words	Synonyms or variations
Part of speech and prefix/suffix/root (as applicable)	**Sketch or symbol**

Written Conversation Note-Catcher

Chapters 22 and 23

Characters have very different reactions in the aftermath of the verdict. How do different characters react? Choose Jem, the black community, Miss Maudie, Bob Ewell, or Dill to write about. What do these reactions reveal about that character or group?

I Say	My Peer Responds	I Build	My Peer Concludes

Text-Dependent Questions Note-Catcher

Chapter 23

Name: _____

Date: _____

Text-Dependent Questions	Response using the strongest evidence from the text
1. What does Atticus's reaction to Bob Ewell's threats and name-calling reveal about his character?	
2. Atticus says, "Jem, see if you can stand in Bob Ewell's shoes a minute. I destroyed his last shred of credibility at that trial, if he had any to begin with. The man had to have some kind of comeback, his kind always does. So, if spitting in my face and threatening me saved Mayella Ewell one extra beating, that's something I'll gladly take. He had to take it out on somebody and I'd rather it be me than that houseful of children. You understand?" (218). How does his explanation relate to the Golden Rule?	

3. "Atticus tells Jem, 'As you grow older, you'll see white men cheat black men every day of your life, but let me tell you something and don't you forget it—whenever a white man does that to a black man, no matter who he is, how rich he is, or how fine a family he comes from, that white man is trash.'

Atticus was speaking so quietly his last word crashed on our ears. I looked up, and his face was vehement. 'There's nothing more sickening to me than a low-grade white man who'll take advantage of a Negro's ignorance. Don't fool yourselves—it's all adding up and one of these days we're going to pay the bill for it. I hope it's not in your children's time'" (221).

Why is Atticus so vehement?

What do you think Atticus means when he says "it's all adding up"?

4. "'Tom's jury sho' made up its mind in a hurry,' Jem muttered.

Atticus's fingers went to his watchpocket. 'No it didn't,' he said, more to himself than to us. 'That was the one thing that made me think, well, this may be the shadow of a beginning. That jury took a few hours. An inevitable verdict, maybe, but usually it takes 'em just a few minutes" (222).

What does Atticus mean by "shadow of a beginning"? Beginning of what? Explain.

5. When discussing choosing a Cunningham for the jury, Atticus says, "When you analyze it, there was little risk. There's no difference between one man who's going to convict and another man who's going to convict, is there? There's a faint difference between a man who's going to convict and a man who's a little disturbed in his mind, isn't there?" (223).

What does he mean that there was little risk? What does this illustrate about Atticus's belief in his fellow human beings?

To Kill a Mockingbird Structured Notes Graphic Organizer

Chapters 24–26

Name: _____

Date: _____

Chapter 24 (227–234) Summary

As September inches closer, Scout is introduced to formal teatime, hosted by Aunt Alexandra, who is on a relentless campaign to teach her to be a lady. As Scout navigates through the social hour, she's lost on how ladies can look so pretty and delicate and yet trap each other with conversation, revealing an aggressiveness you can't really see except when they talk to each other. She decides she feels much more at home in her father's world.

What's the gist of pages 234–237?

What's the gist of chapters 25 and 26?

Focus Question

What are two things the reader learns about Atticus's character in these chapters? Use the strongest evidence from the novel to support your answer.

EXPEDITIONARY
LEARNING

Vocabulary

Word	Definition	Context clues: How did you figure out this word?
scowling (238)		
remorse (242)		
recluse (242)		
spurious (244)		
persecute (247)		

Integrity: Frayer Model

Name: _____

Date: _____

Definition	**Characteristics/Explanation**
Examples	**Nonexamples**

EXPEDITIONARY
LEARNING

Key Quotes

Name: _____

Date: _____

Directions: Read the example of a character taking a stand on the sentence strip. Choose one of the four quotes that best demonstrates the category of the stand you've been given. Write a brief explanation for why you think the example fits under that quote.

A. "Mockingbirds don't do one thing but make music for us to enjoy. They don't eat up people's gardens, don't nest in corncribs, they don't do one thing but sing their hearts out for us. That's why it's a sin to kill a mockingbird" (90).

_____

_____

_____

_____

B. "You never really understand a person until you consider things from his point of view—until you climb into his skin and walk around in it" (30).

_____

_____

_____

_____

C. "I wanted you to see what real courage is, instead of getting the idea that courage is a man with a gun in his hand. It's when you know you're licked before you begin but you begin anyway and you see it through no matter what. You rarely win, but sometimes you do" (112).

_____

_____

_____

_____

_____

D.   "Before I can live with other folks I've got to live with myself. The one thing that doesn't abide by majority rule is a person's conscience" (105).

_____

_____

_____

_____

_____

EXPEDITIONARY
LEARNING

Exit Ticket

Name: _____

Date: _____

How is taking a stand related to integrity? Explain.

_____

_____

_____

_____

_____

_____

_____

_____

_____

_____

_____

_____

_____

_____

_____

_____

_____

_____

_____

_____

_____

To Kill a Mockingbird Structured Notes Graphic Organizer

Chapter 27

Name: _____

Date: _____

What is the gist of what you read?

Focus Question

Reread Atticus's explanation of Bob Ewell's actions on page 251, beginning with "I think I understand . . ." and ending with "Atticus chuckled." What does Atticus's explanation reveal about his character? Use the strongest evidence from the novel to support your answer.

Vocabulary

Word	Definition	Context clues: How did you figure out this word?
industry (248)		
notoriety (248)		
obscure (248)		
eccentricities (250)		

To Kill a Mockingbird Model Essay

Essay prompt: **When Mrs. Dubose dies, Atticus says, "It's when you know you're licked before you begin but you begin anyway and you see it through no matter what" (112). Does it make sense for Mrs. Dubose to take a stand for herself? Give evidence from the text to support your thinking, and be sure to take into account what people who disagree might say.**

Mrs. Henry Lafayette Dubose is a grumpy old woman who lives down the street from the Finches in Harper Lee's *To Kill a Mockingbird.* She spends her days in bed but sometimes sits on her porch in her wheelchair and yells at Jem and Scout as they walk by. Despite her rough exterior, Mrs. Dubose takes a stand for herself, determined to overcome a morphine addiction before she dies. Because of her high expectations for herself and her courage, it makes sense for Mrs. Dubose to take that stand.

The first reason it makes sense for Mrs. Dubose to take a stand is that she has high expectations for people, including herself. When Jem and Scout walk by her house, Mrs. Dubose does not let any small transgression go by without commenting on it. For instance, Scout says, "If I said as sunnily as I could, 'Hey, Mrs. Dubose,' I would receive for an answer, 'Don't you say hey to me you ugly girl! You say good afternoon, Mrs. Dubose!'" (99). This shows that Mrs. Dubose holds high expectations of others, even if they make a small mistake. Just as she has high expectations for Scout and Jem's behavior, she has high expectations of herself. After her death, Atticus reports, "She said she was going to leave this world beholden to nothing and nobody" (111). This shows that Mrs. Dubose means to hold herself to the kind of expectations that she holds others to, even if it is going to be very difficult for her.

The second reason it makes sense for Mrs. Dubose to take a stand is her courage. As Atticus says to Jem, Mrs. Dubose is in a lot of pain. "Most of the time you were reading to her, I doubt if she heard a word you said. Her whole mind and body were concentrated on that alarm clock" (111). This shows that Mrs. Dubose needs to find a way to keep her mind off the pain. The fact that she is successful shows how brave she is. Atticus says to Jem: "I wanted you to see something about her—I wanted you to see what real courage is, instead of getting the idea that courage is a man with a gun in his hand. . . . She was the bravest person I ever knew" (112). This demonstrates that Mrs. Dubose has a lot of courage, even though she seems so hateful. Mrs. Dubose shows courage by taking a stand for herself.

Some might say that it does not make sense for Mrs. Dubose to take this stand. It is true that her decision to overcome her addiction increases her pain. As Atticus says about her morphine addiction, "She'd have spent the rest of her life on it and died without so much agony, but she was too contrary" (111). This shows that it was agony to get herself off morphine. However, that reinforces the idea that Mrs. Dubose is, in fact, a brave woman. If she tolerates pain to die how she wants to, it means that she is courageous. Therefore, it does make sense for Mrs. Dubose to take that stand.

It is clear that Mrs. Dubose's decision to take a stand for herself makes sense. She holds herself to the same high expectations that she holds others to. Mrs. Dubose is also very brave and faces pain and suffering to take her stand. Mrs. Dubose shows how important it is to stand up for yourself, even "when you know you're licked before you begin but you begin anyway and you see it through no matter what" (112).

Supporting Evidence-Based Claims Graphic Organizer

Body Paragraph 1

Reason 1:

Evidence	Evidence	Evidence
How does this evidence support this reason?	How does this evidence support this reason?	How does this evidence support this reason?

Body Paragraph 2

Reason 1:

Evidence	Evidence	Evidence
How does this evidence support this reason?	How does this evidence support this reason?	How does this evidence support this reason?

Body Paragraph 3

Reason 1:

Reason for counterclaim:

Evidence	Evidence	Evidence
How does this evidence support this reason?	How does this evidence support this reason?	Why is your claim stronger than this counterclaim?

Source: Adapted from Odell Education.

Exit Ticket

Name: _____

Date: _____

Directions: Read the essay prompt.

Atticus says, "Simply because we were licked a hundred years before we started is no reason for us not to try to win" (chapter 9, page 76). Now that you have read the whole text, what do you think? Does it make sense for Atticus to take a stand to defend Tom Robinson? Give evidence from the text to support your thinking, and be sure to take into account what people who disagree might say.

1.   What will you need to do before you begin writing to address the prompt well in your essay?

_____

_____

_____

_____

_____

_____

_____

_____

_____

_____

_____

_____

_____

_____

_____

_____

_____

_____

_____

To Kill a Mockingbird Structured Notes Graphic Organizer

Chapter 28

Name: _____

Date: _____

What is the gist of what you read?

Focus Question

How does Harper Lee build suspense in this chapter? Use the strongest details from the novel to support your answer.

Vocabulary

Word	Definition	Context clues: How did you figure out this word?
irascible (255)		
gait (255)		
pinioned (262)		
staccato (263)		
untrammeled (266)		

End-of-Unit 2 Assessment Prompt

To Kill a Mockingbird Argument Essay

Atticus says, "Simply because we were licked a hundred years before we started is no reason for us not to try to win" (chapter 9, page 76). Now that you have read the whole text, what do you think? Does it make sense for Atticus to take a stand to defend Tom Robinson? Give evidence from the text to support your thinking, and be sure to take into account what people who disagree might say.

_____

_____

_____

_____

_____

_____

_____

_____

_____

_____

_____

_____

_____

_____

_____

_____

_____

_____

_____

_____

_____

EXPEDITIONARY
LEARNING

Supporting Evidence-Based Claims Graphic Organizer

Body Paragraph 1

Reason 1:

Evidence	Evidence	Evidence
How does this evidence support this reason?	*How does this evidence support this reason?*	*How does this evidence support this reason?*

Body Paragraph 2

Reason 1:

Evidence	Evidence	Evidence
How does this evidence support this reason?	*How does this evidence support this reason?*	*How does this evidence support this reason?*

Body Paragraph 3

Reason 1:

Reason for counterclaim:

Evidence	Evidence	Evidence
How does this evidence support this reason?	*How does this evidence support this reason?*	*Why is your claim stronger than this counterclaim?*

Source: Adapted from Odell Education.

Exit Ticket

Name: _____

Date: _____

1. What is your claim about Atticus's decision to defend Tom Robinson?

    _____

    _____

    _____

2. Which reasons will you use to support your claim?

    _____

    _____

    _____

3. Which counterclaim will you include in your essay?

    _____

    _____

    _____

To Kill a Mockingbird Structured Notes Graphic Organizer

Chapters 29, 30, and 31

Name: _____

Date: _____

What is the gist of what you read?

Focus Question

What does Scout mean when she says, "Atticus was right. One time he said you never really know a man until you stand in his shoes and walk around in them. Just standing on the Radley porch was enough"? Use the strongest details from the novel to support your answer.

Vocabulary

Word	Definition	Context clues: How did you figure out this word?
reprimand (270)		
blandly (271)		
eluded (273)		
connived (273)		

To Kill a Mockingbird Argument Rubric

Criteria	CCSS	4	3	2	1	0
CLAIM AND REASONS: The extent to which the essay conveys complex ideas and information clearly and accurately to logically support the author's argument	• W.2 • R.1–9	• Clearly introduces the text and the claim in a manner that is compelling and follows logically from the task and purpose • Claim and reasons demonstrate insightful analysis of the text(s) • Acknowledges and responds to counterclaim(s) skillfully and smoothly	• Clearly introduces the text and the claim in a manner that follows from the task and purpose • Claim and reasons demonstrate grade-appropriate analysis of the text(s) • Acknowledges and responds to counterclaim(s) appropriately and clearly	• Introduces the text and the claim in a manner that follows generally from the task and purpose • Claim and reasons demonstrate a literal comprehension of the text(s) • Acknowledges and responds to counterclaim(s), but the thinking isn't clear or logical	• Introduces the text and the claim in a manner that does not logically follow from the task and purpose • Claim and reasons demonstrate little understanding of the text(s) • Does not acknowledge or respond to counterclaim(s)	• Claim and reasons demonstrate a lack of comprehension of the text(s) or task

Criteria	CCSS	4	3	2	1	0
COMMAND OF EVIDENCE: the extent to which the essay presents evidence from the provided texts to support the argument	• W.9 • R.1–9	• Develops the argument (claim and reasons) with relevant, well-chosen facts, definitions, concrete details, quotations, or other information and examples from the text(s) • Sustains the use of varied, relevant evidence • Skillfully and logically explains how evidence supports the claim and reasons	• Develops the argument (claim and reasons) with relevant facts, definitions, details, quotations, or other information and examples from the text(s) • Sustains the use of relevant evidence, with some lack of variety • Logically explains how evidence supports the claim and reasons	• Partially develops the argument (claim and reasons) of the essay with the use of some textual evidence, some of which may be irrelevant • Uses relevant evidence inconsistently • Sometimes logically explains how evidence supports the claim and reasons	• Demonstrates an attempt to use evidence but only develops ideas with minimal, occasional evidence that is generally invalid or irrelevant • Attempts to explain how evidence supports the claim and reasons	• Provides no evidence or provides evidence that is completely irrelevant • Does not explain how evidence supports the claim and reasons

Criteria	CCSS	4	3	2	1	0
COHERENCE, ORGANIZATION, AND STYLE: the extent to which the essay logically organizes complex ideas, concepts, and information using formal style and precise language	• W.2 • R.1–9	• Exhibits clear organization, with the skillful use of appropriate and varied transitions to create a unified whole and enhance meaning • Establishes and maintains a formal style, using grade-appropriate, stylistically sophisticated language and domain-specific vocabulary with a notable sense of voice • Provides a concluding statement or section that is compelling and follows clearly from the claim and reasons presented	• Exhibits clear organization, with the use of appropriate transitions to create a unified whole • Establishes and maintains a formal style using precise language and domain-specific vocabulary • Provides a concluding statement or section that follows from the claim and reasons presented	• Exhibits some attempt at organization, with inconsistent use of transitions • Establishes but fails to maintain a formal style, with inconsistent use of language and domain-specific vocabulary • Provides a concluding statement or section that generally follows the claim and reasons presented	• Exhibits little attempt at organization, or attempts to organize are irrelevant to the task • Lacks a formal style, using language that is imprecise or inappropriate for the text(s) and task • Provides a concluding statement or section that is illogical or unrelated to the claim and reasons presented	• Exhibits no evidence of organization • Uses language that is predominantly incoherent or copied directly from the text(s) • Does not provide a concluding statement or section

Criteria	CCSS	4	3	2	1	0
CONTROL OF CONVENTIONS: the extent to which the essay demonstrates command of the conventions of standard English grammar, usage, capitalization, punctuation, and spelling	• W.2 • L.1 • L.2	• Demonstrates grade-appropriate command of conventions, with few errors	• Demonstrates grade-appropriate command of conventions, with occasional errors that do not hinder comprehension	• Demonstrates an emerging command of conventions, with some errors that may hinder comprehension	• Demonstrates a lack of command of conventions, with frequent errors that hinder comprehension	• Minimal, making assessment of conventions unreliable

Quote Sandwich Guide

A sandwich is made up of three parts—the bread on top, the filling in the middle, and the bread on the bottom. A "quote sandwich" is similar; it is how you use evidence in an argument essay. First, you introduce a quote by telling your reader where it comes from. Then, you include the quote. Last, you explain how the quote supports your idea. Read this example of using a quote in an argument essay, and then take a look at the graphic:

When Jem and Scout walk by her house, Mrs. Dubose does not let any small transgression go by without commenting on it. For instance, Scout says, "If I said as sunnily as I could, 'Hey, Mrs. Dubose,' I would receive for an answer, 'Don't you say hey to me you ugly girl! You say good afternoon, Mrs. Dubose!'" (99). This shows that Mrs. Dubose holds high expectations of others, even if they make a small mistake.

Introduce the quote.
This includes the "who" and "when" of the quote.
Example: *When Jem and Scout walk by her house, Mrs. Dubose would not let any small transgression go by without commenting on it.*
Sample sentence starters for introducing a quote:

In chapter, _____   _____.
When Scout is _____ , she _____.
After _____ , Atticus _____.

Include the quote.
Make sure to punctuate the quotes correctly, using quotation marks. Remember to cite the page number in parentheses after the quote.

Example: *For instance, Scout says "If I said as sunnily as I could, 'Hey, Mrs. Dubose,' I would receive for an answer, 'Don't you say hey to me you ugly girl! You say good afternoon, Mrs. Dubose!'" (99)*

Analyze the quote.
This is where you explain how the quote supports your idea.
Example: *This shows that Mrs. Dubose holds high expectations of others, even if they make a small mistake.*
Sample sentence starters for quote analysis:

This means that _____.
This shows that _____.
This demonstrates that _____.

EXPEDITIONARY
LEARNING

Quote Sandwich for Peer Critique

Name: _____

Date: _____

Directions: For today's peer critique, look at your Supporting Evidence-Based Claims Graphic Organizer and choose the reason in one of your body paragraphs to focus on. Then choose one piece of evidence from that paragraph to turn into a quote sandwich. Make sure you introduce the quote, include the quote, and explain how the quote supports the reason in that paragraph. Remember that you have practiced quote sandwiches orally and found them in the model essay.

Quote Sandwich for Peer Critique

For the peer critique, you will share your quote sandwich with a peer. Ask your peer to focus on giving you feedback on one of the four following questions:

Feedback Questions

- Does the introduction of the quote give enough background information to understand it?
- Did I punctuate and cite the quote correctly?
- Does the explanation of the quote make sense?
- Did I use the best evidence to support the reason in my body paragraph?

Peer Critique Expectations and Directions

Expectations

Be kind: Treat others with dignity and respect.

Be specific: Focus on why something is good or what, particularly, needs improvement.

Be helpful: The goal is to help everyone improve their work.

Participate: Support each other. Your feedback is valued!

Directions for Peer Critique Pairs

1. Review Claim and Reasons Criteria from columns 1 and 2 of the *To Kill a Mockingbird* Argument Rubric.

2. Give your peer your quote sandwich and point out the feedback question you would most like suggestions about.

3. Read over your peer's quote sandwich.

4. One person shares his or her feedback using phrases such as:

   a. I really liked how you . . .

   b. I wonder . . .

   c. Maybe you could change . . .

5. Author writes it on his or her Peer Critique Recording Form.

6. Author says: "Thank you for _____. My next step will be _____."

7. Switch roles and repeat.

Directions for Revising My Quote Sandwich

1. Decide where you are going to make changes based on the feedback.

2. Revise your quote sandwich in the space provided.

3. Be sure to include changes when planning an essay and apply feedback to other quote sandwiches as appropriate.

Peer Critique Recording Form (Side A)

Name: _____

Date: _____

4	3	2	1	0
• Claim and reasons demonstrate insightful analysis of the text(s) • Acknowledges and responds to counterclaim(s) skillfully and smoothly	• Claim and reasons demonstrate grade-appropriate analysis of the text(s) • Acknowledges and responds to counterclaim(s) appropriately and clearly	• Claim and reasons demonstrate a literal comprehension of the text(s) • Acknowledges and responds to counterclaim(s), but the thinking isn't clear	• Claim and reasons demonstrate little understanding of the text(s) • Does not acknowledge or respond to counterclaim(s)	• Claim and reasons demonstrate a lack of comprehension of the text(s) or task
• Develops the argument (claim and reasons) with relevant, well-chosen facts, definitions, concrete details, quotations, or other information and examples from the text(s) • Sustains the use of varied, relevant evidence • Skillfully and logically explains how evidence supports the claim and reasons	• Develops the argument (claim and reasons) with relevant facts, definitions, details, quotations, or other information and examples from the text(s) • Sustains the use of relevant evidence, with some lack of variety • Logically explains how evidence supports the claim and reasons	• Partially develops the argument (claim and reasons) of the essay with the use of some textual evidence, some of which may be irrelevant • Uses relevant evidence inconsistently • Sometimes logically explains how evidence supports the claim and reasons	• Demonstrates an attempt to use evidence but only develops ideas with minimal, occasional evidence that is generally invalid or irrelevant • Attempts to explain how evidence supports the claim and reasons	• Provides no evidence or provides evidence that is completely irrelevant • Does not explain how evidence supports the claim and reasons

EXPEDITIONARY
LEARNING

Peer Critique Recording Form (Side B)

Name: _____

Date: _____

Focus of Critique: Quote Sandwich
My peer thinks the best thing about my quote sandwich is . . .
My peer wondered about . . .
My peer suggested I . . .
My next step(s) . . .

EXPEDITIONARY
LEARNING

To Kill a Mockingbird Essay Planner

Name: _____

Date: _____

Focus Question: Does it make sense for Atticus to defend Tom Robinson?

I. Introduction

A. Hook to capture the reader's interest and attention	
B. Name the book and author	
C. Give brief background information to the reader about the book (characters, plot overview, etc.)	
D. Claim	

II. Body Paragraph 1

First reason to support your claim	
A. Topic sentence	
B. Quote sandwich 1	
C. Quote sandwich 2	

D. Quote sandwich 3	
Concluding sentence	

III. Body Paragraph 2

Second reason to support your claim	
A. Topic sentence	
B. Quote sandwich 1	
C. Quote sandwich 2	
D. Quote sandwich 3	
Concluding sentence	

IV. Body Paragraph 3

Counterclaim	
A. Topic sentence	
B. Reason to support counterclaim	

C. Quote sandwich 1	
D. Quote sandwich 2	
E. Response to counterclaim	
F. Explanation of response to counterclaim	
G. Concluding sentence	

V. Conclusion

A. Restate claim	
B. Summarize reasons	
C. Explain why your view is worth consideration by the reader	

Writing Improvement Tracker

Name: _____

Date: _____

Strategies to Improve Writing

- Revise my writing (or my planning) multiple times
- Look at other models
- Read others' work
- Ask questions when I have them
- Take a break and reread with fresh eyes

- Ask myself, "Does this make sense?"
- Read the necessary texts closely
- Talk through my ideas with an adult
- Use quote sandwiches
- Have another student write the gist of my paragraphs and make sure they match what I think they are

Essay from Module 1

Directions: Look at the first two rows of the Grades 6–8 Expository Writing Evaluation Rubric.

1. What do I do well in my essay?

_____

_____

2. What do I need to improve?

_____

_____

3. What is my goal for the next module for those areas? (Be specific. "I will do better" is too general. Name a specific skill to improve, such as "I will use stronger evidence in my writing.")

_____

_____

4. Look at the list of strategies at the top of this tracker. What one or two strategies will I use to meet my goal in the next module?

_____

_____

Essay from Module 2

Directions: Look at the first two rows of the Grades 6–8 Expository Writing Evaluation Rubric.

1. What do I do well in my essay?

_____

_____

2. What do I need to improve?

_____

_____

3. What is my goal for the next module for those areas? (Be specific. "I will do better" is too general. Name a specific skill to improve, such as "I will use stronger evidence in my writing.")

_____

_____

4. Look at the list of strategies at the top of this tracker. What one or two strategies will I use to meet my goal in the next module?

_____

_____

EXPEDITIONARY
LEARNING

Essay from Module 3

Directions: Look at the first two rows of the Grades 6–8 Expository Writing Evaluation Rubric.

1.   What do I do well in my essay?

_____

_____

2.   What do I need to improve?

_____

_____

3.   What is my goal for the next module for those areas? (Be specific. "I will do better" is too general. Name a specific skill to improve, such as "I will use stronger evidence in my writing.")

_____

_____

4.   Look at the list of strategies at the top of this tracker. What one or two strategies will I use to meet my goal in the next module?

_____

_____

Position Paper from Module 4

Directions: Look at the first two rows of the Argument Writing rubric.

1.   What do I do well in my essay?

_____

_____

2.   What in my writing improved this year?

_____

_____

3. Which strategy helped me the most?

_____

_____

4. Which improvement am I most proud of?

_____

_____

End-of-Unit 2 Assessment Prompt

To Kill a Mockingbird Argument Essay

Atticus says, "Simply because we were licked a hundred years before we started is no reason for us not to try to win" (chapter 9, page 76). Now that you have read the whole text, what do you think? Does it make sense for Atticus to take a stand to defend Tom Robinson? Give evidence from the text to support your thinking, and be sure to take into account what people who disagree might say.

Performance Task Prompt

After reading *To Kill a Mockingbird,* analyze key quotes that reflect the overarching central ideas or themes studied in Units 1 and 2. In a small group, you will develop a Readers Theater script based on your group's quote. Your group will develop the script by selecting critical scenes from the novel that develop the central idea expressed in the quote. On your own, you also will write two pieces: a justification (Mid-Unit 3 Assessment) to explain how the scenes your group selected help develop the main idea of the quote, and a commentary (End-of-Unit 3 Assessment) to explain how your group's script is a response to *To Kill a Mockingbird* and how it connects to and diverges from the novel.

Key Quotes

(Each quote is spoken by Atticus.)

A. "Mockingbirds don't do one thing but make music for us to enjoy. They don't eat up people's gardens, don't nest in corncribs, they don't do one thing but sing their hearts out for us. That's why it's a sin to kill a mockingbird." (90)

B. "You never really understand a person until you consider things from his point of view—until you climb into his skin and walk around in it." (30)

C. "I wanted you to see what real courage is, instead of getting the idea that courage is a man with a gun in his hand. It's when you know you're licked before you begin but you begin anyway and you see it through no matter what. You rarely win, but sometimes you do." (112)

D. "Before I can live with other folks I've got to live with myself. The one thing that doesn't abide by majority rule is a person's conscience." (105)

Part 1: Individual Scripting

Each member will write an individual narrative "passage script" from the novel relating to the key quote provided to your group. On your own, you will choose a scene from the novel that develops the main idea of your key quote. Along with that, you will write narration that introduces that passage and a short commentary that explains how the passage develops the main idea of the key quote.

Part 2: Group Scripting

You will collaborate with your small group to produce one longer script that connects each person's passage in chronological order, as it happens in the book. When you work as a group, you will focus on making sure the passages flow together: You will refine each person's narration, add transitions, and work as a group to write a conclusion to the group's script. You also will choose props and plan blocking for your performance and rehearse as a group. Your group will perform your final high-quality narrative script for the class or school or community members.

Model Readers Theater One-Scene Script

Key Quote

"As I made my way home, I thought Jem and I would get grown but there wasn't much else left for us to learn, except possibly algebra."

Theme

Growing up is about more than just getting older—it is about understanding people and their actions and recognizing that the world doesn't always work as you want it to or think it should.

Roles

Narrator

Jem

Atticus

Miss Maudie

Script

Narrator: Jem has realized that Atticus had a reason for not bragging about his talent. Jem wants to be like his father, and so you can see he is beginning to grow up. By the time he turns 12, he is difficult to live with, inconsistent, and moody. But his loss of innocence has barely begun when he, Scout, and Dill sneak into Tom Robinson's trial and listen intently as the witnesses give their testimony. After the jury leaves to deliberate, Jem is confident.

Jem: Don't fret; we've won it. Don't see how any jury could convict on what we heard.

Narrator: Jem truly believes that people will do the right thing and find Tom innocent. Until the jury found him guilty.

Jem: Atticus—

Atticus: *(Moving closer to Jem and putting his hand on Jem's shoulder)* What, son?

Jem: How could they do it? How could they?

Atticus: I don't know, but they did it. They've done it before and they did it tonight and they'll do it again, and when they do it—seems that only children weep. Good night.

Atticus walks away.

Narrator: The next day, Miss Maudie invites Jem, Scout, and Dill over for some cake.

Miss Maudie: Don't fret, Jem. Things are never as bad as they seem.

Jem: It's like bein' a caterpillar in a cocoon, that's what it is. Like somethin' asleep wrapped up in a warm place. I always thought Maycomb folks were the best folks in the world—least that's what they seemed like.

Miss Maudie: We're the safest folks in the world. We're so rarely called on to be Christians, but when we are, we've got men like Atticus to go for us.

Jem: *(grinning ruefully)* Wish the rest of the county thought that.

Miss Maudie: You'd be surprised how many of us do.

Jem: *(starting to sound angry)* Who? Who in this town did one thing to help Tom Robinson, just who?

Miss Maudie: His colored friends, for one thing. And people like us. People like Judge Taylor. People like Mr. Heck Tate. Stop eating and start thinking, Jem. Did it ever strike you that Judge Taylor naming Atticus to defend that boy was no accident? That Judge Taylor might have had his reasons for naming him?

Narrator: This was a thought. Court-appointed defenses were usually given to Maxwell Green, Maycomb's latest addition to the bar, who needed the experience. Maxwell Green should have had Tom Robinson's case.

Miss Maudie: You think about that. It was no accident. I was sittin' there on the porch last night, waiting. I waited and waited to see you all come down the sidewalk, and as I waited I thought, Atticus Finch won't win, he can't win, but he's the only man in these parts who can keep a jury out so long in a case like that. And I thought to myself, well, we're making a step—it's just a baby step, but it's a step.

EXPEDITIONARY
LEARNING

Exit Ticket

My Key Quote and Scene

Name: _____

Date: _____

What is the key quote that has been allocated to your group?

_____

_____

_____

What is the key scene that has been allocated to your group?

_____

_____

_____

EXPEDITIONARY
LEARNING

Mid-Unit Assessment

Readers Theater Scene Selection: Justification

Name: _____

Date: _____

What is your key quote?

_____

_____

_____

Which scene did you choose to communicate this quote?

_____

_____

_____

Why did you choose that scene?

_____

_____

_____

_____

How does your script communicate the key quote?

_____

_____

_____

_____

_____

Peer Critique Guidelines

1. **Be kind:** Always treat others with dignity and respect. This means we never use words that are hurtful, including sarcasm.

2. **Be specific:** Focus on particular strengths and weaknesses rather than making general comments, such as "It's good" or "I like it." Provide insight into why it is good or what, specifically, you like about it.

3. **Be helpful:** The goal is to contribute positively to the individual or the group, not simply to be heard. Echoing the thoughts of others or cleverly pointing out details that are irrelevant wastes time.

4. **Participate:** Peer critique is a process to support each other, and your feedback is valued.

Stars and Steps

Name: _____

Date: _____

Star 1:

_____

_____

_____

Step 1:

_____

_____

_____

Star 2:

_____

_____

_____

Step 2:

_____

_____

_____

Suggestions to help answer question:

_____

_____

_____

Transition Model

End of Scene 1

Narrator: After the whole business with Boo Radley, Bob Ewell, and Tom Robinson was all over, Scout reflected.

Scout: As I made my way home, I thought Jem and I would get grown, but there wasn't much else left for us to learn, except possibly algebra.

Narrator: "What did she mean by that?" you might ask. She meant that she and Jem learned an awful lot about people. They did not see the world like little kids anymore, as they did before the whole mess began.

Scene 2

Narrator: A few weeks later, it was the first day of school for Scout. Jem condescended to take Scout to school the first day, a job usually done by the parents. Some money changed hands in this transaction, for as Jem and Scout trotted around the corner past the Radley place, you could hear an unfamiliar jingle in Jem's pockets.

Model Script Conclusion

Key Quote

"As I made my way home, I thought Jem and I would get grown but there wasn't much else left for us to learn, except possibly algebra."

Theme

Growing up is about more than just getting older—it is about understanding people and their actions and recognizing that the world doesn't always work as you want it to or think it should.

Narrator

Jem has grown up, not just in years but in maturity. Unlike at the beginning, he is now taking care of Scout instead of avoiding her. He now understands more about people and why they do the things that they do, like Atticus and Boo Radley, even if he doesn't always agree with their actions. Jem has learned that the world is more complicated than he used to think.

Venn Diagram

Similarities and Differences between the Readers Theater Script and *To Kill a Mockingbird*

Name: _____

Date: _____

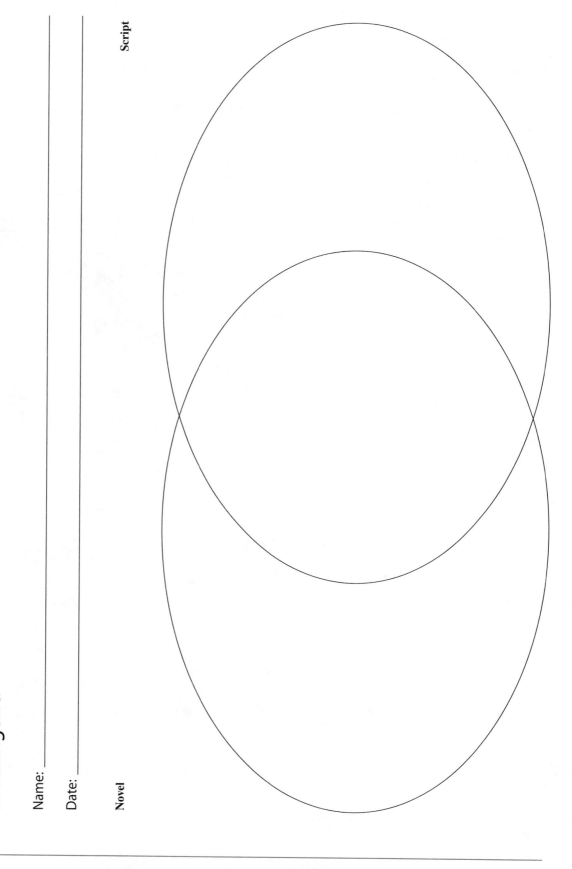

Script

Novel

End-of-Unit 3 Assessment

Readers Theater Commentary

Write a commentary to accompany your group Readers Theater script to answer the following questions:

- "How is your Readers Theater script a response to the novel *To Kill a Mockingbird?*"

- "How does your script connect with the novel? Why?"

- "How does it diverge from the novel? Why?"

Use evidence from the novel and your script to justify your answers. Your commentary should be no more than three paragraphs long.

Row 1 of Readers Theater Rubric

Name: _____

Date: _____

Individual Scores	1–Needs Improvement	2–Fair	3–Good	4–Excellent
Delivery	Student had difficulty reading the script and consistently did not use expression, eye contact, or props appropriately.	Student read the script but had little expression, few gestures, little eye contact, or did not use props appropriately.	Student read the script with some expression, gestures, eye contact, and use of props.	Student read the script with confidence and expression, made gestures and good eye contact, and used props to add to the performance.

Readers Theater Rubric

Name: _____

Date: _____

Individual Scores	1–Needs Improvement	2–Fair	3–Good	4–Excellent
Delivery	Student had difficulty reading the script and consistently did not use expression, eye contact, or props appropriately.	Student read the script but had little expression, few gestures, little eye contact, or did not use props appropriately.	Student read the script with some expression, gestures, eye contact, and use of props.	Student read the script with confidence and expression, made gestures and good eye contact, and used props to add to the performance.
Cooperation with group	Student did not work cooperatively together with the group and could not agree on what to do. Student did not share responsibilities or ideas and wasted time.	Student worked cooperatively with the group in some aspects of the project but sometimes could not agree on what to do and wasted time.	Student worked cooperatively with the group in most aspects of the project and shared most responsibilities and ideas.	Student worked cooperatively with the group in all aspects of the project and shared all responsibilities and ideas well.

Group Members: _____

Group Scores	1–Needs Improvement	2–Fair	3–Good	4–Excellent
On-task participation	Low level of active participation from majority of group members	Moderate level of on-task work or few of the group members actively participating	Majority of group members on task and actively participating	High level of active, on-task participation from all group members

Readers Theater Rubric Self-Assessment

Explain why you gave yourself the score you did for each category.

Delivery: I gave myself a score of _____ (1, 2, 3, or 4) because:

_____

_____

_____

Cooperation with Group: I gave myself a score of _____ (1, 2, 3, or 4) because:

_____

_____

_____

On-Task Participation: I gave myself a score of _____ (1, 2, 3, or 4) because:

_____

_____

_____

I took a nap because I was tired